Myths That Shaped Our History

Myths That Shaped Our History
From Magna Carta to the Battle of Britain

Simon Webb

PEN & SWORD HISTORY

First published in Great Britain in 2017 by
Pen & Sword History
an imprint of
Pen & Sword Books Ltd
47 Church Street
Barnsley
South Yorkshire
S70 2AS

ISBN 978 1 47389 593 5

Printed and bound in England
by CPI Group (UK) Ltd, Croydon, CR0 4YY

Pen & Sword Books Ltd incorporates the imprints of Pen & Sword Archaeology,
Atlas, Aviation, Battleground, Discovery, Family History, History, Maritime,
Military, Naval, Politics, Railways, Select, Social History, Transport, True
Crime, and Claymore Press, Frontline Books, Leo Cooper, Praetorian Press,
Remember When, Seaforth Publishing and Wharncliffe.

For a complete list of Pen & Sword titles please contact
PEN & SWORD BOOKS LIMITED
47 Church Street, (Barnsley: South Yorkshire, S70 2AS, England
E-mail: enquiries@pen-and-sword.co.uk
Website: www.pen-and-sword.co.uk

Contents

List of Plates

1. Queen Victoria and Prince Albert as medieval monarchs.
2. A bad-tempered King John reluctantly signs the Magna Carta.
3. The White Man's Burden: bringing British values to the world.
4. Fundamental British values; supposedly derived from the Magna Carta.
5. The real Henry V; not a bit like Laurence Olivier or Kenneth Branagh.
6. The mud of both the Western Front and Agincourt.
7. Henry V's chivalry in action; prisoners of war having their throats cut.
8. Francis Drake playing bowls; a towering figure in British mythology.
9. Commemorative plaque on the house in South London once occupied by 'Captain' Bligh.
10. 'Captain' Bligh and some of his crew are cast adrift in a small boat, following the mutiny on the *Bounty*.
11. Marshal Blücher, the true victor at Waterloo.
12. The 'Nightingale Rose'; Florence Nightingale's real achievement was in statistics, rather than nursing.
13. The suffragettes as helpless victims, rather than dangerous terrorists.
14. The authentic face of the suffragettes; newspaper reports of bomb attacks in 1913.
15. The popular image of Edwardian Britain; wealthy ladies at Ascot in 1905.
16. The reality of Edwardian Britain; lines of soldiers advance on strikers, as police follow in an armoured car.
17. Over the top; British troops march across No Man's Land towards the waiting German machine guns.
18. General Haig; callous butcher or brilliant strategist?
19. A Spitfire from the Battle of Britain, piloted by a Polish airman.
20. One of the Chain Home radar towers which were of crucial importance during the Battle of Britain.

Introduction: The Meaning of Myth

In everyday usage, the word 'myth' is now almost synonymous with 'misconception' or even 'lie'. When we describe something as a myth, we are in effect saying that it is untrue. We are in this way robbed of a very useful word with a specific meaning quite unconnected with falsehood or truth; which is unfortunate. Some myths are of course untrue; others though are no more than straightforward and accurate historical accounts. Perhaps it would help to understand this if we first cleared the ground a little by thinking about the nature of myth. Only then will we be able to make sense of the subject-matter of this book, which is an account of some of the great myths of British history.

Myths are stories or narratives which help us to make sense of the world and understand our place in it. Sometimes they are tales about the creation of the world. Other myths describe the origin of a nation, religion or ethnic group. In the book of Genesis, the Bible gives a mythical account of the creation of the world. The ancient Romans had a set of myths which told of the founding of their city. The Hindus and Jews both have collections of myths which describe where they come from and explain their association with a particular geographical region. A body of myths or stories which have a meaning for a particular culture in this way is sometimes called a mythos.

The Jewish mythos is to be found primarily in the first part of the Bible; known in Hebrew as the *Tanakh* and to Christians as the Old Testament. For the Hindus, the *Mahabharata* is a mythos which tells of gods and men in the early history of the Indian subcontinent. The British too have their own mythos; a collection of myths which explains who they are and how they came to hold the values and beliefs which they now have. These have never been codified into one definitive book like the Bible, but they have nevertheless given us, among other things, the 'British Values' which successive British governments have in recent years been so keen to promote.

The mythos of the Jews tells them that they are a special people, chosen by God to bear a message to humanity. The mythos of the British is in some ways similar to this, only without the divine commission. Britain, according to this reading of history, is where the principle of the rule of law arose, as well as being the birthplace of modern democracy. These ideals were exported to the rest of the world, giving nations such as the United States of America their core values in the process. No wonder that the Magna Carta Memorial at Runnymede was erected by the American Bar Association. The granite pillar there is inscribed with the words 'To commemorate Magna Carta, symbol of freedom under law'. For America, freedom under law is something which originated in Britain. This gives the British their most popular and enduring mythic narrative, although there are others which are almost as powerful.

Carl Jung popularized the idea of mythic archetypes, recurring figures which crop up in myth systems around the world, such as the hero, the trickster and the wise old woman. He wrote also of archetypal motifs such as the Deluge. Universal floods are to be found not only in the Bible, but also in legends of the Sumerians. Ancient American cultures, such as the Maya and Aztecs, also feature this motif of the worldwide deluge which destroys all humanity other than a tiny handful of survivors. There are also mythic characters and situations which are not universal, but are rather limited to one particular culture. In the Bible, Israel's apostasy is a recurring theme, as is the idea of the prophet without honour in his own land. Jesus Christ is of course the most commonly-known example of this figure from Hebrew myth. The British have their own special set of mythic images and we see these cropping up over and over again in the nation's history.

That the rule of law, habeus corpus and so on have something to do with the Magna Carta and are Britain's most precious gift to the world, is one myth beloved by the British. Others include the myth that Britain does best when outnumbered and with its back to the wall. This David and Goliath image, with Britain battling, and ultimately triumphing, in the face of over-whelming odds is tremendously popular. We see it in the Battle of Agincourt and the defeat of the Spanish Armada. More recent examples of this partic-ular myth come from the Second World War. The evacuation of Dunkirk, the Battle of Britain and the Blitz all show Britain standing alone against a mighty foe and, in the end, coming out on top.

The image of David and Goliath shows how myths can act as a unify-ing force for a nation. When Winston Churchill appealed to the nation's fondness for this particular myth in 1940, he was consciously summoning up the memory of Agincourt by talking of 'the few' to whom so much was owed. The reference was of course to 'we few, we happy few' from Henry V's speech before Agincourt, in Shakespeare's play. Myth can act as a rallying cry.

It is very important to remember that when we talk of these historical events as 'myths', that we are not saying that they did not happen. Certainly, most of them have been dreadfully exaggerated and edited until we are left with a story which bears little resemblance to the original incidents, but that is not always the case. The familiar account of the British retreat from Dunkirk is historically accurate, but it is no less an example of the 'David and Goliath' myth for that.

What then is the point of these myths? Why do religions, ethnic groups and secular societies create and perpetuate myths about themselves? There are two reasons. In the first place, myths give the members of a group an identity and enable them to make claims about themselves. However downtrodden they might be, at least they are chosen by God or are the heirs of some ancient tradition. Britain might today be quite insignificant upon the world stage, but the country's inhabitants can hold their heads up proudly and recall that it was their country which bequeathed to America and other countries their fundamental values. Myths are a way of allowing ordinary people to feel a bit special. Even if they have not done very much themselves, as individuals, they can take pride in the supposed past achievements of their race, culture or nation.

There is another reason that myths are valuable and that is that they enable us to make sense of history, whether our own or that of other cultures. History in the raw is chaotic and messy, consisting of a series of largely random and meaningless episodes. Myths give us a framework which helps us to interpret the past and turn it into a coherent narrative. If I were to ask readers what happened in 1066, for instance, everybody would know at once that this was the year that the Saxon rule of England ended and the Normans took over. William the Conqueror landed and fought a battle at Hastings against Harold, who was the last of the Saxon kings. After Harold was defeated and killed, William went to London where he was crowned. This is the generally accepted sequence of the Norman Conquest, the one which we learn at school.

The Battle of Hastings fits neatly into another mythic narrative of the British Isles, which might be termed the 'Invaders from the East'. Periodically, invaders from the east threaten to overrun Britain. Sometimes, they succeed. We think of the Celts who landed in southern England centuries before Julius Caesar. Then in 55 BC, Caesar brought troops across the Channel and a hundred years later, the Romans occupied a large part of Britain. Five hundred years after that, it was the turn of the Angles, Jutes and Saxons who took over the country in successive waves. After them came the Normans, followed in 1588 by the threat of invasion from Spain. Other manifestations of this myth are to be found in the prospect of Napoleon crossing the Channel in the early nineteenth century, the Battle of Britain in 1940 and then, during the Cold War, the fear that the Russians might sweep in from the east and take over Europe, including of course, Britain. Current fears about a supposed flood of migrants resonate with the British precisely because this too raises the spectre of marauders crossing the Channel.

Seeing 1066 in the context of an overarching myth in this way makes it easier to understand and once we have selected a few facts and discarded others, we are left with a neat story of 'the last successful invasion of Britain', 'the last Saxon king' and so on. The account, as it is usually related, bears little resemblance to the historical record, but that hardly matters. Harold was not the last Saxon king at all: he was succeeded by Edgar Aethling, of whom few people have ever heard. Nor do most people know about the later Battle of London and other military engagements which took place after Harold's death. The important point is that we have a memorable and compact narrative which fits perfectly into the structure of a popular myth cycle about invaders from the east.

In this book, we shall be examining ten myths which have helped to shape the way in which the British see themselves. These ten historical episodes fall into various categories, three of which we have already looked at briefly: Britain as bringer of law and democracy, Britain as target of invaders from the East and Britain as the small country facing a mighty and invincible foe. To these may be added Britain as the nation which saves Europe from itself. These myth-types are not mutually exclusive and in some cases overlap. The Battle of Britain, for instance, shares elements of the invaders from the East, Britain saving Europe and also Britain as a small country standing alone against a mighty enemy. In the same way, the Battle of Waterloo is both about Britain saving Europe from a tyrant whom other countries seem unable to defeat by themselves, but also about bringing democracy and the rule of law to other, less enlightened nations.

Another favourite British myth is the little person standing up against authority. This is similar to, but slightly different from, the David and Goliath myth. In David and Goliath, the less powerful character uses violence to conquer his oppressor. In the little person scenario, the weaker party triumphs by cunning or persistence. It is this image which made the films of Charlie Chaplin such great hits with the British in the early part of the twentieth century. In Chapter 6 we will be looking at the very archetype of the little person struggling against the Establishment, as we examine Florence Nightingale's efforts in the Crimean War.

This brings us to another distinguishing feature of myths, as opposed to mere legends. Myths are narratives or stories, which always feature people, or sometimes gods, as the active forces in the situations of which they tell. In myths, things happen because of the intention of personalities, some human, others supernatural or divine. An ancient story about a natural disaster such as a flood or volcanic eruption is not a myth, but a legend. It might even be plain and unadorned history. The Biblical flood which left only Noah and his family alive, though, is pure myth. This is because it was caused by the agency of Jehovah, as a punishment for the human race's wickedness and depravity. It is this which gives a mythic dimension to the modern take on the flood, rising sea-levels caused by anthropogenic global warming. If this were a purely natural occurrence, it would not grab the imagination as readily as the assertion that the flooding will take place as a result of humanity's profligacy and greed. It is this element, the action of humans, which gives global warming the status of a myth, regardless of whether it is true that the planet actually is heating up or not.

This factor, the desire to attribute natural circumstances and events to the deliberate action of men and women, enables us properly to describe various key passages in British history as 'myths'. The Spanish Armada was scattered and dispersed by the wind, but in the mythic version found in British history books it is the larger-than-life figure of Francis Drake to whom credit is given for this natural event. It is much the same with other incidents, ranging from the rain before Agincourt to the cystitis and piles which afflicted Napoleon at Waterloo and so fatally weakened his judgement. In each of these cases, we attribute victory to noble and determined British warriors, instead of prosaic circumstances which have arisen by the working of blind chance.

The desire to interpret history in terms of kings and queens, soldiers, statesmen and other famous people is an understandable one, but has its perils. Obviously, it is far more interesting to read about Henry VIII and his six wives or the story of Francis Drake finishing his game of bowls before defeating the Armada, than it is to study dry facts and figures relating to the economic, religious and social developments which were really responsible for the upheaval in Europe during the sixteenth century. In a broader sense, we none of us like to feel that we are at the mercy of fate; we all prefer to believe that we are the masters of our own destiny. Viewing history as the product of great men and women's conscious decisions brings order to the chaos and allows us to think that life in general may be controlled, always providing of course that one has a strong enough spirit! The danger is though that in editing historical incidents in order to make it seem as though the driving force of history has been the decisions taken by a handful of important individuals, we are necessarily forced to distort accounts so as to rule out chance and natural circumstances. If we want to see Henry V as the heroic victor at Agincourt, fighting against insurmountable odds of five or six to one, then we must forget the muddy ground upon which his victory was really founded and focus on his noble and stubborn character.

As a direct result of the process outlined above, the ten historical myths at which we will be looking in this book are myths both in the proper sense of being narratives which have special meaning to one particular culture, but also myths in the more commonly-accepted meaning of the word, that is to say largely fictitious. The facts about Waterloo, the generals of the First World War, the suffragettes, Magna Carta and so on bear little or no relation to the stories as they are generally known and understood.

We begin with what might almost be described as Britain's foundation myth: the story of the birth of democracy and the rule of law. Magna Carta is of tremendous importance in British history, because it provided the justification for the very existence of Britain's colonial ambitions and the establishment of the greatest empire the world has ever seen. This first chapter will also introduce us to another great mythic theme in British history; the yearning for a supposedly 'golden age', when everything was much better than it is today. This particular myth is still, as it has been for many centuries, an important one in understanding the psyche of the British people. It explains why so many people in the country still feel an aching nostalgia for various periods of the past, whether this is 'before the war' or, more recently, the 1960s and 1970s.

Chapter 1

Magna Carta 1215:
'The great cornerstone in England's temple of liberty'?

Britain was not founded or created at any particular moment, nor was there any event which marked definitely its becoming a nation, such as the signing of a declaration of independence. Instead, the British have the Magna Carta. Before Magna Carta, there are a few memorable dates such as 55 BC and 1066 AD, along with a handful of notable kings such as Alfred the Great, William the Conqueror and Richard the Lionheart. These rulers seemed to do pretty much as they pleased. From 1215 onwards though, following King John placing his seal on the great charter which the barons presented to him, we know that we have been living in a nation where the rule of law is paramount. Even the monarch is bound by the law to respect the rights of his or her subjects.

Most of us think that we know the story of the Magna Carta, how the barons grew tired of King John's arbitrary rule and the way in which he was riding roughshod over ancient liberties and oppressing the common people. They put together a set of principles, including habeus corpus, which guaranteed that from then on every person in the kingdom would have the right to a fair trial and nobody could be detained without a just cause. In fact if there is one thing most people know about Magna Carta, it is that it stops people being locked up without recourse to the courts. Isn't that what habeus corpus is all about? That the Magna Carta was actually a reactionary document, specifically devised to deny ordinary people any rights and to reverse progressive changes made in the law some years earlier, sounds shocking and even absurd to modern ears. Before going any further, it might be helpful to look at the popular image of the events at Runnymede 800 years ago, just to remind ourselves of what we think we know about the matter. In other words, before examining the historical fact, let us look first at the myth, as we have received it today.

Our ideas about the Magna Carta are usually drawn not from historical or contemporary sources, but rather from a nineteenth-century reimagining of what took place at Runnymede on 15 June 1215. The version of Magna Carta with which we are most of us familiar might not inaptly be called a romantic narrative or, less charitably, a Victorian fairy story. The affection which the Victorians developed for Magna Carta, and which led to their creating an alternative version of reality, had two chief origins, one romantic and the other a desire to mask the brutal *realpolitik* of colonial exploitation.

As the less attractive aspects of the Industrial Revolution, by-products such as urban slums and ugly factories with their chimneys belching forth smoke, became increasingly plain to see, there were attempts in nineteenth-century Britain to create an imaginary past. This showed, to begin with, in a revival of Gothic architecture: new buildings such as railway stations and law courts were designed in a conscious effort to hark back to another age. Even provincial town halls were tricked out to look like cathedrals or fairy-tale castles. The Palace of Westminster in London, more commonly known as the Houses of Parliament, is a magnificent example of what became known as the Gothic Revival style of building. The towers and pinnacles of this iconic building were deliberately designed to look archaic and centuries out of date. Later on, there was a craze for everything to do with the Middle Ages. The Pre-Raphaelite Brotherhood of artists was founded. They and their followers turned out paintings of an idealized medieval world, much of it based upon the legends of King Arthur and his court at Camelot. The Poet Laureate, Alfred Lord Tennyson, turned the medieval epic of Mallory's *Mort d'Arthur* into verse and dedicated the *Idylls of the King* to Queen Victoria. She and her husband posed for paintings and statues in which they were depicted in fancy dress to represent historical figures from the medieval period. Landseer, for example, painted them as the fourteenth-century monarchs Edward III and Queen Philippa. Illustration 1 shows a sculpture of Victoria and Albert as medieval monarchs.

The uncertainties of the Victorian Age found an antidote in the supposedly more pious and chivalrous era between the Norman Conquest and the Tudors. Life in those days was portrayed as being gentler and having more noble values than those of the counting house and wharf, rampant commercialism being blamed for many of the ills of nineteenth-century society. There was a yearning for a pastoral way of life, before industry had taken over and the cities of Britain expanded to bursting point and beyond. William Morris and the Arts and Crafts movement fixed upon the fourteenth century as the epitome of this vanished golden age, designing wallpaper, furniture and textiles to fit in with this fantasy world.

It was as part of this romantic movement that Magna Carta emerged as a talisman or touchstone which symbolized all that was good about England and, by extension, Britain. Instead of the preoccupation with the mercenary and mercantile world of trade which characterized Victorian Britain, the myth grew that there had once been a time when ideals of justice and concern for the rights of ordinary men and women had been the motivating force in the country's history. Powerful men in those days had been prepared to go to war with the king to ensure that the liberty of his subjects was respected and that everybody was entitled to redress in the courts and protection from unjust imprisonment and so on. This version of events was enthusiastically taken up by artists and writers and we cannot do better than look at one or two examples from the time to see how the Magna Carta became known to everybody in nineteenth century Britain as the country's supreme creation, which was destined to be Britain's gift to the whole world.

Three Men in a Boat, by Jerome K. Jerome, is known today as a light-hearted comic novel about the misadventures of a group of middle-class men taking a short holiday by hiring a boat and rowing up the Thames from Kingston towards its source. Apart from the farcical anecdotes for which the book is famous, there are a number of descriptive passages about historical events, including the signing of the Magna Carta. Jerome's take on what took place at Runnymede eight centuries ago encapsulates the myth at which we are looking. The barons are fierce protectors of the rights of the general populace and force King John to accede to their demands on behalf of the people of England. He is reluctant to do so, wishing to hang on to his autocratic rule:

> But the heart of John sinks before the stern faces of the English fighting men, and the arm of King John drops back onto his rein, and he dismounts and takes his seat in the foremost barge. And the Barons follow in, with each mailed hand upon the sword-hilt, and the word is given to let go. Slowly, the heavy, bright-decked barges leave the shore of Runnymede. Slowly against the swift current they work their ponderous way, till, with a low grumble, they grate against the bank of the little island that from this day will bear the name of Magna Charta Island.
>
> And King John has stepped upon the shore, and we wait in breathless silence till a great shout cleaves the air and the great cornerstone of England's temple of liberty has, now we know, been firmly laid.

One almost imagines this seminal incident from English history being depicted in a Pre-Raphaelite painting, so vivid is the imagery. We turn now

to a quintessentially English poet of roughly the same era to give his version
of the meaning of Runnymede. Kipling's *Reeds at Runnymede* was commissioned for C. L. R. Fletcher's *A History of England*. This book was written
for children, thus ensuring that the rising generation in Edwardian Britain
would imbibe the Magna Carta myth in its purest and most distilled form.
It would be tedious to quote this poem in its entirety, but a few extracts will
give the flavour of the thing:

> When through our ranks the Barons came,
> With little thought of praise or blame,
> But resolute to play the game,
> They lumbered up to Runnymede,
>
> At Runnymede, at Runnymede
> Your rights were won at Runnymede!
> No freeman shall be fined or bound,
> Or dispossessed of freehold ground,
> Except by lawful judgement found,
> And passed upon him by his peers,
> Forget not after all these years,
> The Charter Signed at Runnymede.

The marvellous and almost surreal notion of all those medieval barons 'playing
the game', like boys in *Tom Brown's Schooldays*, is an enchanting one! Illustration
2 shows King John signing the Magna Carta. Of course, as any schoolboy knows,
he actually placed his seal upon it, rather than signing his name.

Magna Carta had of course been known to politicians and lawyers for
centuries, but it was the Victorians who brought it to the forefront of the
national consciousness, so that by the end of the nineteenth century, most
people in the country had heard of it and were aware of its supposed significance. Throughout the twentieth century, this universal familiarity
became entrenched, so that in 1959, when an episode of the radio comedy
series *Hancock's Half Hour* was broadcast, Tony Hancock's immortal line,
'Does Magna Carta mean nothing to you? Did she die in vain?', was seen as
wildly amusing. The joke only works of course if everybody listening may
be assumed to know at the very least that Magna Carta was a document and
not a person.

There was a little more to the propagation of the idea of the Magna Carta
as some kind of bill of rights than met the eye. It was not just a handful of
artists and writers peddling the story of the sturdy barons standing up to a

bad king who were responsible for the myth taking off in such a spectacular fashion that even now, almost 200 years later, we still cling to this weirdly distorted view of history. All the romanticizing of the medieval period and the fetishisation of the Magna Carta itself had a strong business end to it, that was used to justify imperialist expansion, not only by the British in India and Africa, but also by the United States as they spread their influence west across their own country and then over the Pacific Ocean.

There is a great irony in the idea of the Magna Carta being exploited for the purposes of colonialism, particularly since the admiration accorded to it had been inextricably bound up in the vision of a chivalrous past, before the modern world became obsessed and preoccupied with industry and trade. Nevertheless, that is precisely what happened. Burgeoning industrial nations essentially require two things: sources of cheap raw materials and ever-expanding markets for their manufactured goods. Colonialism provided Britain with both. Palm oil, wood, rubber and gold were transported from Africa and in return the products of factories in Birmingham and Sheffield were exported and sold to colonists and natives. It was upon the profit from these transactions that Britain's prosperity during Queen Victoria's reign was founded. Put like this, colonialism sounds, as indeed it was, like the systematic exploitation of the weak and powerless by the strong and unscrupulous. This was an unpalatable view for the respectable Victorians – few of us wish to see ourselves as tyrants and oppressors. So it was that the myth of the 'White Man's Burden' came into being, the dishonest claim that occupying and looting the lands of others was some kind of philanthropic enterprise. In both Britain and America, a soothing fiction was devised to assuage the consciences of those who would otherwise baulk at theft and the expropriation of property on an industrial scale. It was to the Magna Carta that those responsible for this self-delusion turned.

The thesis advanced on both sides of the Atlantic Ocean was that white people, especially the British and Americans, had somehow acquired a sacred mission to bring light and the benefits of civilization to those whose skin was darker or more sallow than the average European. In America, this fraud went by the name of 'Manifest Destiny' and it was first outlined by the journalist John L. Sullivan in 1845 when he wrote of 'Our manifest destiny to overspread and to possess the whole of the continent which Providence has given us for the development of the great experiment of liberty and federated self-government entrusted to us'. In short, the ideals of Magna Carta, that is to say democracy and the rule of law, gave America carte blanche to seize any territory they wished to occupy, on the grounds that their own political and social system was manifestly or obviously better than any which might be encountered during this expansion west. Later on in the nineteenth century, this drive west continued across the Pacific until America was imposing its ideals of liberty on nations such as the Philippines, which lay on the edge of the South China Sea.

The American acquisition of the Philippines in 1898, following the Spanish-American War, prompted Rudyard Kipling to write a poem which endorsed the American attitude and also, by implication, that of the British as they forced their way south into Africa. The name of this poem, *The White Man's Burden*, has become notorious as summing up all that was wrongheaded about the Victorian world-view. Dated 1899 and containing a dedication to, 'The United States and the Philippine Islands', it begins

> Take up the White Man's burden -
> Send forth the best ye breed -
> Go bind your sons to exile
> To serve your captives' needs
> To wait in heavy harness
> On fluttered folk and wild -
> Your new-caught, sullen peoples
> Half devil and half child.

Two things immediately strike us when reading this opening verse (there are a further six, with which I shall not burden the reader). The first is the overt claim that colonization, specifically that being undertaken by America at that time but by implication also Britain's similar actions, is undertaken for the benefit of the indigenous inhabitants of whichever land is so favoured. Talk of the 'burden', along with references to 'exile', 'serving' and 'heavy harness' make this perfectly clear. The aim of the enterprise is to raise up those who are less civilized than Britain and America and teach them to live by our values. What are these values? Why, they are none other than those that we imagine to be found in the Magna Carta; individual liberty, freedom of speech, trial by jury and so forth.

The second point which we observe is the contemptuous way that the natives of the Philippines are dismissed as 'fluttered folk and wild' and also, 'half devil and half child'. It is plain that the values and ideals of the 'White Man' cannot fail to be superior to any beliefs held by such people. In this way, the act of transmitting Western values by invading and occupying hot countries laying closer to the equator than our own, becomes not an exercise in rapacity and greed, but rather a noble crusade to raise up those less fortunate than ourselves. It was here that the Magna Carta came in very useful indeed. Illustration 3 shows the 'White Man's Burden', as John Bull and Uncle Sam struggle to carry black and Asian people towards civilization.

We have so far looked at the myth of Magna Carta, that is to say the mistaken view which most of us have of it. It is time now to look at what the Magna Carta actually *was*. If it was not a sacred text guaranteeing ordinary citizens rights under law and protecting them from tyranny, then what was it? To understand that, we must look at the age which produced it and try to work out the motives of those who put it together. Let us begin with that great icon of British values, habeus corpus, which literally means in Latin, 'You have the body'. This is the legal principle which protects us from arbitrary arrest and unlawful imprisonment by the government. It was much discussed when Tony Blair's government was trying to increase the length of time for which suspected terrorists were being held. It was hoped to be able to extend their detention without trial to ninety days, whereupon many people, both inside and outside Parliament, raised the cry of 'Habeus corpus' and the proposal was defeated.

The first thing we need to know is that habeus corpus does not really have anything at all to do with Magna Carta. It originated fifty years earlier, in 1166, the very year that King John was born. The monarch at that time was Henry II and when he came to the throne in 1154, England was recovering from a civil war between King Stephen and the Empress Mathilda. Both sides had hired mercenaries and when the war ended, these men became robbers and brigands, threatening to cause a complete breakdown of law and order throughout the whole country. Many barons ruled their lands as though they were answerable to no one, not even the king. There was also the problem of what amounted to a parallel realm operating within Henry II's kingdom. This was the Church. In the twelfth century, a sixth of England's population were clergy of one sort of another, including many monks and nuns. The Church was jealous of its special status and tried to prevent the Crown from having any jurisdiction over the clergy.

Henry was determined to reassert royal authority over everybody in the realm, whether barons or bishops. How this worked out as regards the clergy may be seen in the unfortunate death of Thomas á Becket in 1170. When he found that he was dealing with a particularly recalcitrant Archbishop of Canterbury, one who was determined to defend the rights of the Church, Henry simply had him murdered. Dealing with the barons was more tricky, because Henry had no wish to precipitate another civil war and the barons were fiercely protective of what they saw as their 'rights'. Eroding the power of the barons would need to be done by more indirect methods. One way of achieving this end was by establishing a new legal system, whereby judges appointed by the king himself travelled around the country, dispensing justice.

At the beginning of Henry's reign, in the aftermath of the bitter civil war, some of the barons had built castles without permission and were behaving as though they were a law unto themselves, inflicting punishments or imprisoning people according to their individual whims. After moving against these men, who threatened the unity of the realm, the king set about reforming the law through declarations such as the Assize of Clarendon in 1166 and the Assize of Northampton, ten years later. These set out a new series of rules which wrested power from the barons and placed it in the hands of the king's judges, who would travel around the country dispensing justice. This was a very unpopular move with the barons; reducing their authority as it did.

In the humorous classic *1066 And All That*, it is said that the barons had many important duties, one of which was 'keeping up the Middle Ages'. This was in fact no more than the literal truth, because keeping up the Middle Ages was precisely what the barons wished to do. The idea that the way in which society was then constituted might in any way be imperfect was anathema to the English nobility. When King John continued the process of depriving them of their 'rights' and bleeding them dry financially into the bargain, the barons revolted. Taxation by the Crown had been a sore point for years and John was extorting six times as much to pay for his foreign wars than his brother Richard had ever done. A rebellion began, the aim of which was partly to reduce the financial burden being laid upon the barons and also to roll back some of the reforms of the last few decades. In short, to take power back from the king.

There were only a few dozen barons in the whole country and in order to gain the support of the rest of the population, it would be necessary for them to represent themselves as fighting for the rights of ordinary people, not just their own mercenary self-interest. To this end, the barons put together a long document which set out what they claimed was an attempt to save the common people from being oppressed by the king. It was in reality nothing of the sort. All but one or two of the sixty-three clauses in the charter had been devised with the privilege of the powerful men opposing King John in mind. Some of it though was so cunningly worded that it might, at first sight, have appeared to be an appeal made on behalf of the farmers, workers and citizens of England. This long and complicated list of demands became known as the Magna Carta and the intention was to persuade King John to put his seal to it. Although 'Magna Carta' is usually translated as 'great charter', it was really only given this title because of its great length, not because there was anything momentous about it. Its aim was nothing less than to restore the power of the barons at the expense of everybody else in the country.

It is time to look in detail at what the Magna Carta did and did not offer to the English people. Anybody who has not actually read the thing, and that includes the overwhelming majority of people in this country, might have the vague idea that the Magna Carta is something along the lines of the United Nations Universal Declaration of Human Rights. Nothing could be further from the truth and the plain fact is that 99 per cent of the famous charter has no conceivable relevance for anybody who is not actually living in the Middle Ages! One or two examples might serve to illustrate this point. Let us look at Clause 57:

> In cases where a Welshman was deprive or dispossessed of any-thing, without the lawful judgement of his equals, by our father King Henry or our brother King Richard, and it remains in our hands or is held by others under our warranty, we shall have respite for the period commonly allowed to crusaders, unless a lawsuit had been begun, or an enquiry had been made at our order, before we took the cross as a crusader. But on our return from the crusade, or if we abandon it, we will at once do full justice according to the laws of Wales and the said regions.

Unless you are a Welshman living at the time of the Crusades, it has to be said that this clause is not likely to have any bearing on your day-to-day life. Other clauses are equally meaningless to anybody not at war with the King of England during the thirteenth century. Clause 59 begins, 'With regard to the return of the sisters and hostages of King Alexander of Scotland...', and Clause 33 calls for the removal of fish weirs from the Thames and the Medway. So it goes on for sixty-three clauses, with nothing relating to any-thing other than the concerns of rich landowners in medieval England.

Almost the whole of the Magna Carta is taken up with matters relating to the social structure at that time of the barons and the Church. These concern taxes and inheritance and would not have affected the man and woman in the street in any way. Sometimes this is disguised, in order to make it appear that the charter offered some benefit to the ordinary citizen. For instance, one clause promises that the king will, 'Restore lands, castles, liberties and rights to anyone from whom we have unjustly taken them.' In this context of course, 'liberties and rights' have reference only to property and inheritance rights, which for the average man in early thirteenth-century England would have been wholly irrelevant.

Other clauses appear at first sight to offer some benefit to those other than the barons and their families, but one must look very hard for these and sift patiently through an awful lot of dross to find these one or two specks of gold. Before looking at these, we must consider something about society at that time which is often overlooked and this is the division between 'free' and 'unfree' people. About half the population of England in 1215, at the time that the Magna Carta was issued, were 'villeins'. These were men and women who were tied to the land and who could not move from their homes without the permission of their landlord. Their position was roughly analogous to that of the serfs in Imperial Russia. If they were not quite slaves, they were certainly not in any sense free. This section of the population rates hardly any mention at all in Magna Carta, the needs and rights of half the people living in the country at that time were irrelevant. The class is mentioned just once, in a clause which says that 'a fine imposed on a villein must not deprive him of the means to carry on farming', a move which was in the interest of the landed gentry, rather than the villein, because a tenant farmer who was unable to farm would be little use to a landlord. Apart from this single reference, there is a vaguely worded requirement that 'all subjects of the realm' should benefit from the 'customs and liberties' contained in the Magna Carta. Since there was no mechanism to enforce this, the statement was meaningless.

This then was the charter which was presented to King John at Runnymede, during a truce in the armed struggle between the monarch and his barons. From the very opening clause, which was addressed to, 'all the free men in our realm', Magna Carta was specifically directed towards the benefit of the wealthy and free, not the ordinary peasant, bound to his master's land. The first fourteen clauses dealt only with questions of taxation and property rights, which were of little interest even to the 'free' men whom the charter would supposedly benefit. Not until Clause 39 do we reach the bits which supposedly form the basis for our modern-day writs of habeus corpus. Once again, these specifically exclude half the people in the country at that time;

No free man shall be seized or imprisoned, or stripped of his rights or possessions, or outlawed or exiled, or be deprived of his standing in any way, nor will we proceed with force against him, or send others to do so, except by lawful judgement of his equals or by the law of the land.

The following clause goes on to assert that, 'to no man will we sell, to no one deny or delay justice'.

As we have seen, this notion, that people would not be arbitrarily imprisoned, without recourse to the law, was really introduced not in the Magna Carta, but almost fifty years earlier in the Assize of Clarendon. It was this attempt to take charge of the legal system and bring the administration of justice under centralized control, which caused such anger among the barons and led, in the fullness of time, to the struggle between King John and his barons. Readers might wonder why, if the barons disliked the idea of the monarch taking charge of the courts and administering the law, that a clause guaranteeing access to justice should have been inserted into the charter which they presented to the king. The answer is simple.

To gain the support of the free citizens, the barons had at least to appear to be fighting for their interests, as well as their own. Inserting clauses promising benefits to 'all free men' was a great way of achieving this end. In May 1215, the month before King John agreed to the terms of the Magna Carta, the City of London opened its gates to the rebels, so impressed were they with the supposed advantages of siding with the barons against the king. Of course, there was more to it all than met the eye. The real purpose of the charter was not to give anybody other than the rebellious nobles any power. They hoped to do away with the king's authority entirely. One of the clauses made provision that:

> The barons shall choose twenty-five of their number who with all their might shall ensure that the peace and liberties granted by our charter are properly observed and maintained

It went on to say, 'Anyone in the land who wishes may take an oath to obey the twenty-five'.

What was really being planned was that the barons themselves should take over the country and administer it in any way they saw fit. Justice would be doled out according to the old customs and the reforms instituted by Henry II would be swept away. This charter would have made feudalism the way of life in Britain for as long as the barons remained strong. For most people, this would be worse than living even under a corrupt and greedy monarch like John, and for the villeins, it would mean that their freedom was officially crushed for the foreseeable future. It was a document practically guaranteed to divide the realm and provoke a civil war. Had its provisions been adopted in full, it would have meant the end of any sort of freedom for at least half the men and women of England.

The meeting at Runnymede, where King John agreed to issue the Magna Carta in his own name, was followed shortly afterwards by the resumption of war with the barons. After John's death in 1216, his nine-year-old son Henry became king, although rule was delegated to a regent. Two revised versions of the Magna Carta were issued in October and November of that year. The barons were defeated the following year and in 1225, yet another revision of the Magna Carta was made. In 1264 and 1297, there were further issues, each leaving out more and more of the original charter. Often, when people today quote from the Magna Carta, it is not the document agreed by King John to which they refer, but one of these later revisions.

Anybody who knew nothing of the almost superstitious reverence in which the Magna Carta is held, both in this country or abroad, and read it for the first time, would probably not see that it had any particular relevance to the modern world. Such a person would be perfectly correct in forming this view, as even the legal system of the United Kingdom has acknowledged over the years. In spite of the fact that many people still somehow have the notion that the Magna Carta is the foundation upon which our entire legal system is built and indeed is part of the edifice which makes Britain distinct from other countries, very few realize that it has over the years been more or less abolished and no longer has any legal standing. All but three of the original sixty-three clauses have been crossed out and two of those are of no interest to most people.

The original Magna Carta was issued in June 1215 and revised five times before the end of the thirteenth century. By that time, it had been reduced to just thirty-seven clauses. In that truncated form, it remained as the law of the land until 1829, when George IV agreed to repeal Clause 26. Another fifteen clauses were removed under the provisions of the Statute Law Revision Act of 1863 and also the Statute Law (Ireland) Revision Act of 1872. By the end of Victoria's reign in in 1901, another six clauses had been removed.

The last revision of the Magna Carta took place in 1969, when six more clauses were lopped off, leaving just three remaining clauses. All this might come as a bit of shock to those who have the idea that this venerable document is somehow sacrosanct and still of enormous importance to the true-born citizen of Britain! The three clauses which remain on the Statute Book are as follows:

Clause 1: First, we have granted to God, and by this our present charter have confirmed, for Us and Our heirs for ever, that the Church of England shall be free, and shall have all her whole rights and liberties inviolable. We have granted also, and given to all the free men of our realm, for Us and Our heirs for ever, these liberties under-written, to have and to hold to them and their heirs, of Us and Our heirs for ever.

Clause 13: The City of London shall have all the old liberties and customs. Furthermore We will and grant, that all other cities, boroughs, towns, and the barons of the five ports, and all other ports, shall have all their liberties and free customs.

Clause 39: No free man shall be taken or imprisoned, or be disseised of his Freehold, or liberties, or free customs, or be outlawed, or exiled, or any otherwise destroyed; nor will We not pass upon him, nor condemn him, except by lawful judgement of his peers, or by the law of the land. We will sell to no man, we will not deny or defer to any man either justice or right.

These paragraphs, then, are all that is left of the famous charter and the only parts which have been held to have the remotest importance for Britain today, that the Church of England shall be protected, the City of London held in special regard and, almost as an afterthought, that nobody must be sent to prison unless he has been properly convicted of a crime.

We will see shortly just how much this impressive safeguard actually means in practice, but first we must see how the Magna Carta, which really was only of importance to certain sections of society in medieval England, should have come to have so much significance attached to it today. It is still referred to when debates turn to freedom and protection from wrongful imprisonment. In 2008, when the British government succeeded in increasing the length of time that terrorist suspects could be held from twenty-eight to forty-two days, the then Shadow Home Secretary David Davis resigned as an MP in protest. He mentioned the Magna Carta as being somehow germane to the issue, claiming that it was a document which 'guarantees the fundamental element of British freedom, habeas corpus'. It came as no surprise that somebody would raise Magna Carta at such a time, even though habeas corpus did not actually become part of the statute law of England until the passing of the Habeus Corpus Act of 1679, four and a half centuries after Magna Carta. Invoking this obscure piece of legislation though would not have struck nearly so much a chord as did the mention of Magna Carta!

The Magna Carta as we know it today is largely the creation of the late Elizabethan and Jacobean lawyer, Sir Edward Coke, widely considered to have been the greatest jurist of his age. Coke's career was a glittering one: Solicitor General, Speaker of the House of Commons, Attorney General and author of a seminal work on English law. As Attorney General, Coke led the prosecution of the Earl of Essex for his abortive attempt to depose Elizabeth I and also that of Sir Walter Raleigh and then the Gunpowder Plot conspirators. Following these celebrated cases, he was knighted and then made Chief Justice of the Common Pleas. It is for his writing on the interpretation of the law that Coke is known today, in particular *Institutes of the Lawes of England*, a four-volume work, three volumes of which were published posthumously.

Sir Edward's analysis of the Magna Carta is magnificent and he draws out far more from the raw material of those sixty-three clauses than one would ever guess possible. Where the ordinary person sees references to fish weirs, the Crusades and the sisters of King Alexander of Scotland, Sir Edward Coke was able to find an exposition of the principles of English law dating back to the time before the Norman Conquest of 1066. As he put it, the charter was full of 'great weightinesse and weightie greatness'. Anybody wishing to understand the fundamental principles of English law was advised to sift through the Magna Carta very carefully to see what was to be found there. It is Coke's interpretation of the charter that most of us know about now, rather than the rather dull and uninspiring text to which King John affixed his seal in 1215.

By all of this, it will be seen that the British attachment to what they fondly suppose to be the origin of their values has little to do with the events at Runnymede 800 years ago and more to do with a complex and debatable analysis by an early seventeenth-century jurist. Perhaps the most interesting point about it all is that even the remaining clauses of the Magna Carta promise us precisely nothing at all and will be overruled by any British government which feels in the mood for doing such a thing. In short, it guarantees nothing at all and is of no practical significance, binding the government to nothing at all. As soon as the concept of habeas corpus becomes inconvenient or clashes with the urgent needs of the moment, any British government will drop it like a hot potato. Only a very few instances are needed to show the truth of this assertion. Three from the twentieth century should be sufficient to make the point.

In 1914, following the outbreak of war with Germany, the Defence of the Realm Act was passed. This made provision for the arrest and imprisonment of anybody living in the United Kingdom who had been born in Germany. Thousands of men were detained and held in often poor conditions behind barbed wire in what were openly called at the time 'concentration camps'. One at Camberley in Surrey alone held over 8,000 prisoners. These men had no recourse to law and some were held for over four years.

During the Second World War, an even tougher line was taken by the government of the time. In August 1939, before war had even been declared, Parliament was recalled from its summer recess in order to pass the Emergency Powers (Defence) Act. A notorious provision of this act was 18B, which gave the authorities power to lock up anybody they wanted to, whether British or any other nationality, for as long as they wished. Habeas corpus was suspended without a second thought. Sir Oswald Moseley, the leader of the British Union of Fascists, was perhaps the most famous victim of this legislation, but there were many others; some of them quite prominent men and women. One notable example of the use of this draconian act was the arrest and detention of Norah Elam, the former secretary of the Women's Social and Political Union, more commonly known as the suffragettes. She had been associated with the British Union of Fascists in the 1930s and was as a consequence locked up in Holloway Prison without the right to a trial.

The situation in Northern Ireland was even worse than it was in England. There, the Special Powers Act of 1922 gave the authorities in the province to do whatever they wished, ignoring habeas corpus as any time. When a bombing campaign was launched by the IRA just before the Second World War, the Special Powers Act was used to arrest suspects and hold them indefinitely. On 22 December 1938, thirty-four men were arrested on suspicion of being members of the IRA. These men were not charged with any offence, nor were they brought before a court. Some were not released until after the war had ended. In other words, men were held without access to the courts for seven years in the United Kingdom, without anybody worrying in the least about Magna Carta and habeas corpus!

It may be argued that such cases might be justified during a world war, but there are more recent cases of British governments chucking the Magna Carta overboard when it gets in the way of what is seen as good governance. In 1972, the so-called 'Troubles' in Northern Ireland became so violent that direct rule from Westminster was introduced. A minister in London ran the province and regulated the use of various laws to try and suppress the IRA. On 30 March 1972, the Northern Ireland (Temporary Provisions) Act 1972 received Royal Assent. This meant that the British government assumed complete and direct responsibility for running Northern Ireland's affairs. At once, a problem arose. All the specific legislation relating to Northern Ireland was now set aside, including the 1922 Special Powers Act. This was the legal mechanism which allowed the authorities to detain men without trial. From now on, arrested prisoners would have to be brought before the courts and tried for offences in the same way as they were in the rest of the United Kingdom. This was unthinkable and so William Whitelaw, the first Secretary of State for Northern Ireland, at once and without a second thought, signed the Detention of Terrorists (N.I.) Order 1942 (1972 No. 1632 [NI.15]). This order, which was made under the new Northern Ireland (Temporary Provisions) Act did away with habeas corpus and allowed men to be arrested and held without trial for the rest of their lives if necessary. Nothing more clearly indicates just how meaningless is the lip-service paid to Magna Carta and the ease with which habeas corpus can be disregarded when it is felt to be necessary. A total of 2,000 political prisoners were held under the law passed in 1972 and nobody seemingly even noticed that a coach and horses were being driven through Magna Carta.

This first chapter has been concerned with the Magna Carta because the influence of this charter, or rather the *idea* of the charter, is still an enormously potent one. Under the Counter-Terrorism and Security Act 2015, a duty is laid upon those working in schools and colleges to prevent young people from being drawn into terrorism. One of the ways that this is to be done is by the promotion of 'British Values', those of democracy, individual freedom and the rule of law. Inevitably, Magna Carta is brought out and exhibited as summing up and symbolizing all these British values. Whether discussion in the classroom or lecture theatre turns to voting, obeying the law or freedom of speech, Magna Carta is presented as the font of it all. Illustration 4 shows the fundamental British Values, as prescribed by the government.

From the idea of Britain as the source of democracy and the rule of law, we move to another favourite myth of the British: the image of the country as the underdog, battling against insurmountable odds. This David and Goliath approach to history begins in earnest with an episode in the Hundred Years War against France. Since this was also the period which saw the emergence of Britain as an island nation, the Battle of Agincourt is worth giving particular attention to, as reference to it crops up at critical times in British history, for example in both the First and Second World Wars.

Chapter 2

The Battle of Agincourt 1415:
'We few, we happy few,
we band of brothers'

The Battle of Agincourt, in which a smaller English force won a decisive victory against a French army during the Hundred Years War, casts a long shadow, one which reaches across the centuries. Shakespeare's version of events, which is how we chiefly know of this incident in a long and protracted war, was manipulated to great effect during the Second World War. In 1940 Winston Churchill made conscious reference to Henry V's speech before the battle, which is found of course in the play *Henry V.* The line Shakespeare gave the king, 'we few, we happy few' was the basis for Churchill's reference to the RAF, that 'Never in the field of human conflict was so much owed by so many to so few'. The fighter pilots who took part in the Battle of Britain became known in later years as, 'the Few'. Nor was this the only way in which Agincourt entered the public consciousness at that time. In 1944, towards the end of the war, as Britain was about to embark upon the invasion of Europe, it was felt that a boost for morale wouldn't come amiss. The British government accordingly helped to finance a spectacular, Technicolor film version of *Henry V*, starring Laurence Olivier in the title role. The film shamelessly evoked the spirit of Agincourt by being dedicated to the, 'Commandos and Airborne Troops of Great Britain the spirit of whose ancestors it has humbly been attempted to recapture'.

The spirit of Agincourt was of course famously summoned up during the First World War as well. It is a curious fact that a number of seminal events in British history have taken place within a few miles of each other in an unremarkable area of agricultural land in northern France and Belgium. Agincourt, Waterloo and the great battles of the First World War all occurred here. In late August 1914, the first major engagement of the First World War between the British Expeditionary Force and the German army took place at Mons in Belgium. Although they fought well, the British were forced to retreat. A month later, the British author Arthur Machen published a short story in the London *Evening News*. It was called *The Bowmen* and told the story of how a British soldier at the Battle of Mons had called upon St George and found his unit being protected by phantom archers, the ghosts of the British bowmen from Agincourt.

Machen's story was a convincing, first-person account and readers began writing to the *Evening News*, asking for further details of this miraculous intervention. In vain did Arthur Machen explain that the whole thing was fiction and that he had invented it. By the following Spring, Machen's bowmen had undergone a transformation and were now angelic figures, indicative of the fact that Britain's actions in continental Europe were receiving divine support. In recent years, there has been a resurgence of interest in angels, especially in the United States, and the 'Angels of Mons' have been cited in support of the idea that angels have been documented as involving themselves in human affairs. As was remarked earlier, the Battle of Agincourt casts a very long shadow indeed!

Agincourt works so well upon the British psyche because it evokes three of the nation's most powerful and stirring mythic narratives. On the one hand, it is a very early iteration of the David and Goliath myth in British history and, as such, retains a special place in our hearts. A vastly outnumbered British force faces a huge foreign army which threatens to annihilate it. The British have little going for them, beyond their bravery and belief in the rightness of their cause and this somehow enables them to overcome the odds against them and beat the foe. We will see this image again in the next chapter, when plucky English seadogs defeat the mighty Armada, but Agincourt is the prototype of such encounters, the pattern from which all other versions are cut.

The second mythic image with which the Battle of Agincourt resonates is that of the British going over to Europe and sorting things out for them. We will see this theme again in Chapter 5, which is about Waterloo and also in the final chapter, which explores the Battle of Britain and the Blitz. The British have always been keen to set things right in Europe and show the countries there, principally Germany and France, how they should be conducting their affairs. Agincourt is also the earliest narrative illustrating this myth.

Finally, the Hundred Years War, of which the Battle of Agincourt was a part, marks the birth of Britain's identity as an island nation. Until that time, England had been an integral part of Europe, with the rulers of the country and their barons holding extensive lands in France. Indeed, some kings of England spent more time in France than they did in this country. The end of the Hundred Years War brought all that to a close. Although

England retained Calais, it was agreed that whatever the nominal situation might be, in fact France was no longer under English control. From now on, the British were geographically and nationally separate from Europe.

Historical facts frequently bear little or no relation to the myths which grow up around them. This is certainly true of Agincourt. At the back of our minds, we feel that we have a rough idea of what Henry V was like. We all remember Prince Hal and his laddish behaviour before the death of his father. We know too how he changed for the better once he was king and stopped associating with the dubious pot-companions of his youth. Indeed, his former best friend, Sir John Falstaff, is banished from court because young Henry wishes to change and become a worthy monarch. Later on, the handsome young king goes off to lead an army to victory in France.

The problem with all this is of course that it is taken not from the historical record, but rather from a play. Sir John Falstaff, in the play, is a comic character who provides the light relief with his various japes. Offstage, Falstaff becomes very melancholy after the king rejects him, but that is the worst of it. Falstaff was based upon the real-life friend of Henry V, Sir John Oldcastle. Indeed, in the earliest version of Shakespeare's play, Henry's early companion is actually named as Sir John Oldcastle. It was only after one of Sir John's descendants objected to the use of the name that Shakespeare changed it to Falstaff instead. There can be no better illustration of the difference between the myth as we have received it and the historical facts than the ultimate fate of Henry V's old friend.

One thing which Shakespeare omits from his play is the fact that Henry V was by way of being a religious fanatic, a militant Catholic who resolutely pursued heretics wherever they were to be found. A special target for his persecution were the Lollards, followers of a reforming sect led by John Wycliffe. The Lollards preceded Martin Luther by over a century and were regarded with loathing by devout Catholics. The Lollards' call for the reformation of the Church was rank heresy and Henry's views on this matter were orthodox in the extreme. In the first year of his reign alone, no fewer than seven heretics were burned alive. In the whole of his father's reign, just two men were executed in this way for heresy. Sir John Oldcastle was a Lollard and the fact that he had been Henry V's closest friend in his youth was not sufficient to save him. After some vacillation on the king's part, Sir John Oldcastle was condemned as a heretic and eventually burned alive. His death was especially gruesome, in that he was suspended by chains above the fire and slowly roasted alive. This hardly fits in with our preconceived ideas about Henry and his plucky character! The real Henry V may be seen in Illustration 5.

The climax of the Battle of Agincourt too has one or two surprises for those who only know about it from Shakespeare. Even for the medieval period, Henry's actions were deeply shocking. This was a time when casual brutality in warfare was more or less par for the course and there was of course nothing like the Geneva Convention to inhibit savagery. Nevertheless, Henry's order during the battle to murder all the prisoners held captive by his men was seen as shocking. His archers drew their knives and systematically cut the throats of the helpless men who had earlier surrendered.

It is details like these which never seem to crop up when Agincourt is being brandished as a miraculous victory and Henry V treated as though he were the mirror of chivalry and some kind of ideal medieval monarch. Before looking closely at what really happened at the Battle of Agincourt, rather than what we have heard Kenneth Branagh or Laurence Olivier say on the subject at the cinema or on television, perhaps we should first ask ourselves what an English army was doing in France at that time. In other words, how did a battle come to be fought at Agincourt in the first place?

William the Conqueror came, of course, from France. He was a Norman, one of those whose Viking ancestors had settled on that part of the coast during the ninth and tenth centuries. When William invaded England, this country was not intended to be a replacement for his realm in Normandy, but rather an addition. He wished to be king both of England and also part of France. For the next four or five hundred years, the kings and queens of England therefore regarded themselves as being the legitimate rulers of part, or even the whole, of France. This claim was still going strong as late as the eighteenth century. Queen Anne, for example, who reigned from 1702 to 1714, styled herself, 'Queen of Great Britain, France and Ireland'.

Over the centuries, these Continental possessions gradually shrank, until by the time of Henry VIII, only the town of Calais and some of the surrounding land remained English. It was the Hundred Years War that brought about this state of affairs and it was to reclaim authority over part of France that Henry V went to war in August 1415. After a victory at Harfleur, a city which he captured on 22 September, things went badly wrong for the king and he decided that it would be wise to make a tactical withdrawal to the port of Calais, which was at that time indisputably English territory. This move was prompted by the fact that the French had raised a great army, which was being assembled in Rouen, to the east of Harfleur, combined with the fact that Henry's own army was being reduced by disease. The last thing that Henry wished was to become trapped in Harfleur for a lengthy siege. The French army now ready to engage him was far larger than his own and so the obvious solution was for him to march north and hope to leave France in a hurry and then come back later, with a bigger army of his own. His original dream of perhaps besieging Paris would have to be abandoned, at least for that year.

The Somme is more usually associated in most people's minds with the First World War, rather than the medieval period. Nevertheless, it was to the River Somme that Henry V and his army were heading in October 1415, hoping to cross the river and then move swiftly north to Calais. His army were now desperately tired, many of them suffering from dysentery and running low on rations into the bargain. Their journey took them across what would one day be the battlefields of both the First and Second World Wars. We have all heard of the Somme in connection with the First World War, but not everybody knows that this region is also where Rommel operated during the invasion of France in 1940. One of the spots where Henry's army camped for the night was Hangest, where on 5 June 1940, Rommel crossed the river with his panzers.

The River Somme blocked the path of the retreating army and at the first point where a crossing was attempted, it was found that the French commanded the north bank, making any attempt at crossing fraught with hazard. The British moved along the Somme, finally crossing the river at a village called Voyennes. Once across, three French heralds approached, asking which road Henry and his men would be taking, so that the French might, 'meet thee to fight thee, and be revenged for thy conduct'. When the king replied, 'Straight to Calais, and if our enemies try to disturb us in our journey, it will not be without the utmost peril', this must have sounded like a massive bit of bluffing, both to the French and also his own army. By now, it was clear to everybody that the French had mustered greatly superior numbers of men, including a large body of cavalry.

At this point, Henry's army had marched over 250 miles in just over a fortnight. They were weary and hungry; many were also ill. Shortly after crossing the Somme, scouts brought news that a 'terrible multitude' lay between the British and their destination. There was nothing for it but to fight. Henry opened secret negotiations with the French, with a view to securing free passage to Calais, even offering to return Harfleur, which he had left garrisoned by part of his army. The answer from the leaders of the French army was uncompromising; nothing doing. Their aim was to force battle with their vastly greater forces and inflict as much damage as possible on the English. This is how matters stood as darkness fell on 24 October 1415, the eve of the Feast of Saint Crispin.

We know that Henry V's army was outnumbered by the French, but it is quite impossible after all these years to say just how great was the disparity between the two bodies of armed men. What did that 'terrible multitude' amount to in numbers of soldiers? Estimates range from as low as 5,000, all the way up to 200,000. A reasonable figure, laying somewhere between these two extremes, might be 25,000. The British, for their part, had about 6,000–7,000 men, the majority of whom were archers. On the face of it, this would suggest that Henry's army was outnumbered by four or five to one, but this rough estimate is misleading. The French force contained many more unarmed pages than the British had, and that swelled their numbers. As far as fighting forces were concerned, it is possible that the British were only outnumbered by two or three to one. Even so, the French had the advantage that their troops were fresh and had not just trekked 250 miles on inadequate rations. Nor were the French ranks full of men suffering from, or recovering from, dysentery. To top it all, the French had a great force of cavalry, whereas the English army was made up chiefly of infantry. The outlook was without doubt bleak that night. And then, to cap it, it began to rain. The prospects for the following day looked grim indeed.

The British though had an edge, although few people on that gloomy night could have realized just what a stupendous edge it was: at least two-thirds of their army consisted of men with longbows. The longbow, which probably originated in Wales, was a six-foot bow, made of yew and tipped at either end with horn. They were tremendously hard to pull to their greatest extent, with a draw-weight of somewhere in the region of 100lbs, and had a killing range of over 200 yards. A skilled archer could send upwards of six arrows a minute into the air. These would not usually be fired at specific targets, as in competitive shooting or hunting, but rather fired high into the air, to rain down upon an enemy. No defence was possible against such an assault and even armour did not prevent injury and death from arrows. They could fly through eye holes or mouth slits in helmets quite easily. Henry V himself had a ragged scar on his cheek, acquired when he was campaigning in Wales as a teenager. He had opened the visor of his helmet and an arrow had flown straight through and embedded itself a few inches below his left eye.

Before describing the battle itself, it might be a good idea to dispose of a legend which has grown up in the last few years, to the effect that the obscene 'V' sign, used as a term of abuse by the British, had its roots at Agincourt. The story is that the French at that time were cutting the index and middle fingers from the right hands of English and Welsh prisoners, to prevent them from ever using a longbow again. The archers at Agincourt supposedly brandished these two fingers at the French before the battle in order to show that they at least were still able to fire arrows at them.

The only problem with this story is that there is absolutely no record of it until relatively recently. It is true that one contemporary French source says that Henry warned his men on the night before the battle that the French had threatened to cut two fingers from the right hand of every archer they captured, but that is all. The first definite recorded instance of the 'V' sign being used abusively dates only from 1900 and it was not until the 1950s that it became widespread and common. The Agincourt explanation is a neat and plausible little tale, but without a shred of evidence that it is true.

To understand the disaster that Agincourt became for the French, it is necessary to have some idea of the topography of what would become the battlefield. The road north, which the British army hoped to take to Calais, ran between two thickly wooded areas. At the narrowest point, there was only half a mile between the two forests. All the French army needed to do was sit tight and the British would then be forced to fight if they wished to proceed any further. Nestled in the woodland to the west of the armies was the little village and castle of Agincourt, after which the battle was named.

The defender in medieval warfare always had the advantage and Henry hoped to retain this, by setting up a defensive position and simply waiting for the French to attack. There was no room for fancy manoeuvring on either side. Often during a battle, then as now, each side tries to exploit the enemy's weakness by striking at the flanks or sides of any formation and then perhaps swinging round and attacking from the rear. Nothing of this sort was possible, because of the trees which hemmed in the area where the fighting would be taking place. Only frontal assaults could be undertaken. This meant that the two armies would clash, head to head, and the strongest would gain the victory. Things did not look at all promising for Henry's men.

The torrential rain, which had soaked them relentlessly for hours before the battle and made a miserable night for the troops on both sides, had also worked to give the British an extra edge. On either side of the road were freshly-ploughed fields and these were now very muddy, which would not affect Henry's troops, because they would simply be standing in one spot. It would have grave implications though for the French, who would be obliged to charge through the heavy, waterlogged clay which made up the soil in that area.

The two armies were about a thousand yards apart and on the morning of 25 October, Henry prepared for the fight of his life. The archers had been instructed to cut stakes from trees in the nearby forests and sharpen them at both ends. These were planted in the soil, angled towards the direction from which the attack would come. Then, the British waited. They waited, and then they waited a little more. Four hours passed in this way, with the whole army taut and ready for action. Henry and his commanders knew that they could not afford to wait indefinitely, because if the battle were to be too long delayed, the soldiers, who were already exhausted, would be fit for nothing. And so, with great reluctance, the order was given to uproot the defensive hedge of sharpened stakes and move 200 yards towards the French lines. When this had been done and the new position established, the archers began shooting at the opposing forces, which were now just within range.

The French were goaded into launching their attack. They could not simply stand there and wait for the arrows to begin picking them off and so the cavalry began charging across the fields towards the English lines. Once this happened, the archers speeded up their rate of fire, until an almost unbelievable 40,000 arrows a minute were falling onto the mounted knights who were cantering towards them. Behind the riders came the men on foot, most of whom were wearing plate armour weighing 60lbs or so. Although neither side knew it yet, the stage was now set for one of the most stunning and unexpected reversals of military fortune ever seen.

The horses ridden by the French had armour protecting their heads and chests, but little protection on their flanks. The arrows striking home had the effect of maddening the horses with pain, although seldom killing them outright. The natural consequence was that they bolted in all directions. The cavalry were quite unable to reach the archers and put them out of action, because of the sharpened stakes which faced them. Nor were any riders able to ride round and attack from the side, the trees which hemmed in the battlefield prevented this. The battle thus began badly for the French, but things were to get a good deal worse.

The English were holding the narrowest part of the gap between the two forests which lined the road. This was a space which was 800–900 yards wide from one tree-filled area to the other. A little way along the road north, the distance between the woods grew a little greater. Where the French army was camped, there was 1,200 yards from one lot of trees to the other. This was the length of the French line of knights on foot and there was much jostling to be at the front and thus secure a role in the glorious and overwhelming victory which was expected. As they advanced, of course, the gap narrowed and the 1,200-yard long mass of men on foot was gradually compressed into a space of only 900 yards. It must have been like people moving along a very crowded street, with every man crammed hard against those around him and no room for anybody to change direction or even halt for a second to decide what to do next.

Not only were the footsoldiers crowded together like men shuffling along the platform on the Underground, during the rush hour, but they also had to contend with those 40,000 arrows a minute falling from the sky and whizzing straight towards them. Although they were wearing helmets, this did not make them invulnerable to arrows and in order to protect their faces, the knights bent their heads forward, so as present the armoured tops of their heads to the archers ahead of them. This might have lessened the risk of an arrow flying through an eye hole, but it also made breathing more difficult, as well as making it all but impossible to see where they were going and what lay ahead of them.

One final aspect of the situation must be considered and that is the effect of the previous night's weather. The rain had left the ploughed fields absolutely waterlogged. The clay soil tended to retain water and the space between the two opposing armies was nothing but a sea of mud. This mud had been churned up by the advance of the cavalry and turned to a semi-liquid slurry. To get some idea of the conditions in which the French army was advancing that autumn day, it is only necessary to look at photographs of battlefields in that same area, 500 years later. Illustration 6 shows a battlefield near the River Somme during the First World War. The scenes of muddy desolation through which British troops were compelled to struggle during that time give us a very good picture of what those armour-clad knights faced at Agincourt. In 1916, there were stories of soldiers falling into pools of mud and drowning. Imagine how much worse would be the situation for men wearing heavy armour. At the best of times, a man in full plate armour who fell over would need the assistance of others to get to his feet again. Such help would not be forthcoming in the heat of battle, particularly with the troops crowded together like sardines in a tin.

The tragedy unfolded now with a terrible inevitability. The cavalry who had mounted the first assault on the English lines were out of control. The only way for the frightened horses to run was straight back, into the solid mass of infantry who were now advancing. The crush among the armoured infantry meant that there was no possibility of dodging out of the way of a charging horse. Most of the men on foot would not in any case even have seen a rider approaching. The first intimation of anything out of the ordinary for these hapless individuals would have been when a frantic horse crashed into their line, knocking them to the ground. Once a man had fallen over into the mud, he would have been unable to get up by himself. The sticky mud would have exacerbated the difficulties, making it harder to move. Some of those who fell over that day drowned or suffocated as the mud blocked the breathing holes in their helmets. Imagine falling into one of the pools of water to be seen in Illustration 6, while wearing heavy armour! The same fate befell some on the English side too. The most high-ranking knight to die at Agincourt was the Duke of York, who suffocated as a result, according to a contemporary chronicler, of 'much heat and pressing'.

There was no question really of the French knights even being able to fight the English, there was scarcely room in their ranks to swing a sword. As men fell, so those behind them tripped over their prone bodies. Few of them even reached the enemy, let alone fought them. The English archers darted out, from time to time, to recover arrows for use and to kill those laying helplessly in the mud or to drag them back as prisoners to be ransomed. There was a good business opportunity here as some of the more noble of the knights would fetch a very high sum in exchange for their release.

So far, the battle had not even really begun, in the sense of armed men getting to grips with each other and fighting to see who was stronger or more agile. Had that happened, then the heavily-armoured infantry and cavalry of the French would have triumphed in minutes over the English. They were, however, not even able to get close to their adversaries. The climax of the Battle of Agincourt was fast approaching. The French decided to launch another cavalry charge. This one was doomed from the start, even without all those archers firing at them. The French cavalry rode forward and just before the line of the English forces was reached, they were compelled to halt. There were so many dead knights laying in mounds, that these formed an effectively barrier over which the horses would have been unable to climb. It was a mass of metal, made up of thousands of dead men clad in steel armour. It was while the cavalry were milling about, trying to find a route through the carnage that an episode took place which earned Henry V the nickname 'Cutthroat' in France for centuries to come.

Incredibly, there were some among the French aristocracy who had more important engagements that morning than fighting a battle with the cornered, English army. The Duke of Brabant, for instance, had been attending a christening party and did not arrive on the scene with a group of knights until the second cavalry charge. Not having witnessed the massacre of the flower of French knighthood, he obviously thought that the cavalry, who had come to a halt in front of the wall of corpses, were just shilly-shallying and only needed somebody to give them a bit of encouragement. He saw himself as being just the man for the job and rode forward and began rallying the riders and urging them forward to attack.

There followed a sequence of events which was shocking even to medieval sensibilities, which were a good deal less delicate than our own as far as warfare was concerned. By unhappy coincidence, just as the Duke of Brabant appeared in front of the English, giving perhaps the impression that reinforcements were arriving, a small group of knights accompanied by a number of peasants managed to make their way through the woods to the rear of the English army. The baggage train, which consisted of all the supplies, provisions and other material needed by the army, was in the charge of boys too young actually to fight in the battle. These youngsters were promptly murdered and the baggage train looted.

From Henry's perspective, it must have looked as though the tide of battle might be about to turn in favour of the French. He was facing a new onslaught from the front and now the French had apparently found a way to attack his flanks and rear. It was at this point that he decided that having all those prisoners in the midst of his army was a hazard which he could do without. Suppose that in the mounting chaos, they managed to arm themselves and then start an assault from behind the English lines? The king accordingly gave the order to kill all the prisoners.

There was some reluctance to slaughter the helpless and unarmed men, but this was motivated less by compassion than by purely mercenary self-interest on the part of the English soldiers. Under the English military system, ordinary soldiers were entitled to a share of all ransom extracted for the return of prisoners to their own side. The *Gaignes de Guerre* rule set out in detail how much each soldier might expect to receive. Because many of those taken prisoner during the Battle of Agincourt were knights and noblemen, the monetary gain would have been considerable for every man in Henry's army. There were, according to some accounts, murmurs of protest at the idea of massacring men who might bring the English troops a welcome bonus. Realizing that there was opposition to his plans, Henry threatened to hang any man who disobeyed him in the matter. He assigned an ensign and 200 archers to attend to the matter.

The butchery of the French captives was undertaken in an exceedingly crude fashion, by either cutting the throats of the helpless men or smashing their skulls open. Illustration 7 shows a contemporary painting of a French knight having his throat cut in this way. So urgent was the apparent need to accomplish the killing that there was no time to fool around, removing armour and so on. It was a case of just taking off helmets and then hacking or battering at the unprotected heads and necks. One of the victims of the carnage was the Duke of Brabant, who had been unhorsed during the fighting. There was nothing about his appearance to distinguish him from any other French knight and so the English simply pulled off his helmet and cut his throat.

There was of course no Geneva Convention in the fifteenth century to govern behaviour on the battlefield, but there were definitely accepted rules to which civilized European countries tended to abide, if for no other reason than to ensure that their own prisoners were not badly treated at some later date. There is no way of knowing how many prisoners were disposed of during this bloody episode. It was enough for the French that such a breach of the accepted standards of chivalrous warfare had taken place at all, no matter how many or few men had met such ignominious ends. Years after the battle, Henry V was known in France by the sobriquet of 'Cutthroat'.

When the fighting ended, it was plain to both sides that Henry had won a glorious victory. There are no precise casualty figures, but the French probably lost between 8,000 and 10,000 men. Fewer than 200 English soldiers were killed at Agincourt: some modern writers suggest that the death toll on the English side might have been as low as a hundred. All great battles must have a name of some sort for posterity to remember them by and Agincourt was no exception. As is usually the case, it was for the victor to choose by what name the scene of the fighting should be known to future generations. After the Montjoie, Principal Herald of France, had formally conceded defeat, Henry asked him what the name of the castle was that could be seen towering above the woods. On being told, Henry announced that 'As all battles should bear the name of the fortress nearest to the field on which they are fought, this shall forever be called the Battle of Agincourt.'

Despite being greatly outnumbered, it will be seen that the English at Agincourt had several advantages which were not immediately apparent. Not least of these was the torrential rain which soaked the field of battle the night before the fighting took place. Nobody knows why the British have such an obsessive interest in the weather, but it is curious that the changeable, North Atlantic climate which affects Britain and North-West Europe should have played such a significant role in crucial military engagements through the ages. Agincourt in particular was fought in the same general area as Waterloo and victory in both cases was attributable to the rain on the night before the battles. In the next chapter, we shall see how an existential threat to Britain's national sovereignty was swept away by unseasonable weather, not once but on a number of occasions in the century following Agincourt.

After Agincourt, the British dream of a realm based partly in the island of Britain and partly in France was effectively dead. For good or ill, the nation was, after that day in 1415, destined to be separate and distinct from the continent which lay only a couple of dozen miles from its shores. So strong was this feeling of separation to become after the Battle of Agincourt, that until a few decades ago, nobody in this country would have questioned the notion that Britain was an entirely separate and distinct entity from Europe. Indeed, for many years, Britain by itself was thought, at least by its inhabitants, to be equally important as the rest of Europe put together. One is irresistibly reminded of the Victorian newspaper headline: 'Great Storm in Channel; Continent Cut Off'. The struggle to decide whether Britain is part of Europe or an altogether separate entity will be explored further in the next chapter.

Chapter 3

The Spanish Armada 1588:
'Mars and Neptune seemed to attend him'

Agincourt saw the birth of the myth that the British fight best when outnumbered and with their backs to the wall. The Hundred Years War as a whole, though, marked the emergence of another mythic theme, in that the British began to see themselves as an island nation, an altogether separate entity from Continental Europe. Before this, the people of Britain had always had a foot in both camps, so to speak. When Julius Caesar landed in 55 BC, he noted that the Celtic inhabitants of Britain had many connections with the people who lived in present-day France and Belgium; they spoke the same language, shared a common culture and were constantly travelling back and forth between one country and the other to visit relatives and friends. Later on, after the withdrawal of the Roman legions from Britain in the fifth century of the Common Era, Angles, Saxons, Jutes and Vikings established colonies in Britain. Britain was at that time merely an outpost of Europe and an awful lot of people had family connections in what would one day become the countries of Germany, Sweden and Denmark.

With the Norman Conquest of 1066, Britain became united with Europe in an even closer way. For the next 400 years, England and parts of France were essentially the same country. The idea of Britain as being in some sense different from the rest of Europe would have been incomprehensible during the Plantagenet dynasty. Kings of England often spent more time ruling in France than they did in Britain.

This whole idea has a very topical feel about it, in the aftermath of the referendum which was held in 2016 on Britain's membership of the European Union. Is Britain an independent island nation or is it an integral part of Europe? This, when it came down to it, was the question being debated in the spring of 2016. Before the end of the Hundred Years War; the very question would have seemed meaningless; which is why that period was of such crucial importance in the shaping of British identity.

The Spanish Armada has been evoked over the last half a millennium to symbolize British resistance to the threat from Europe. When the possibility was mooted of an invasion from France during the Napoleonic Wars, the image of Francis Drake repelling the Armada was used to hearten and encourage the British people and assure them that they could withstand a foreign seaborne assault. In the Second World War too, the Armada was cited as an inspiring example of British pluck, when once again the threat of an invasion from the Continent was on the cards. We saw in the last chapter how the victory at Agincourt made an appearance in the public consciousness of the British in both of the twentieth century's world wars and the Spanish Armada is part of the same theme.

One of the reasons that the Spanish Armada exerts such a powerful influence upon the British is that it combines a number of the mythic motifs at which we have been looking. First, there is of course the 'Invaders from the East' idea, a recurring anxiety to people in the British Isles over the last 2,000 years from Julius Caesar to Adolf Hitler. Secondly, the Armada myth embodies the notion of Britain standing alone against an invincible enemy and winning against the odds. This is what we might call the 'David and Goliath' mythic theme. Then too, with the involvement of the English army in the wars in the Netherlands, we see Britain sorting out Europe and lending a hand against an oppressed country. This was of course the ostensible reason for both the First and Second World Wars. Finally, there is that perennial topic of British interest, the weather.

Those from other parts of the world are often baffled at the almost obsessive interest which the British seem to have in their country's weather. It is a subject which crops up constantly when people meet in the street and is also a staple news item; 'Britain to be hotter than Athens this week', 'Cold snap means that country will be colder than Siberia' are popular newspaper headlines throughout the year. One of the reasons that Britain has such a love-hate relationship with its weather system is that wind and rain have proved crucial at various pivotal occasions in the nation's affairs. We saw that the weather at Agincourt was instrumental in delivering a victory to Henry V's army and so too with the defeat of the Spanish Armada, which was caused more by gusts of wind than by the efforts of Sir Francis Drake and his fellow pirates. At Waterloo too, weather would be the deciding factor in a battle of world-historical importance, resulting in vastly increased British influence on European affairs for the next century and a half.

The story of the Spanish Armada, as it is generally understood, constitutes a perfect example of a myth. This is partly because of the elements which I have just mentioned, but also because it is a narrative featuring both human and divine characters. The dashing and devil-may-care hero, Sir Francis Drake, is credited with having tackled a hugely superior fleet of ships and triumphed against them; in defiance of all the odds. At the time, God too was thought to have taken a hand in the battle and helped to complete Drake's victory. This makes the defeat of the Spanish Armada in many ways an archetypal myth of the kind which would not look out of place in the tales of battles found in the Bible, where men, aided by God, scatter their enemies before them.

The last chapter of Britain's territorial association with Europe ended in 1558, with the siege and capture of the French port of Calais. This was the last possession of the English on continental Europe and its loss was hugely symbolic for British identity. Little wonder that on her deathbed, Mary, the queen who had overseen the loss of Calais, allegedly said that, 'When I am dead and cut open, they will find Philip and Calais inscribed on my heart.' From this point on, Britain was on its own and Europe was recognized to be another place, altogether separate from the British Isles.

The political union of Britain and France is one alternative history which never quite came off; another was Britain becoming a part of the Spanish Empire, the original empire of which it was said that the sun never set on. When Philip of Spain married England's Queen Mary in 1554, the two became coequal rulers of England. Both Philip and Mary's images were on coins and had there been issue from the marriage, then their son or daughter would have united the two kingdoms. This too would have resulted in Britain being indissolubly linked to a European country. Nothing came of it though, and with the accession of Elizabeth to the throne of England, it became plain that Britain and Europe were destined, for the foreseeable future to be to separate and distinct things, a situation which was to exist until the British entry to the Common Market in 1973.

Elizabeth I was a staunch Protestant and after her sister Mary's death set about reinstituting the church which her father had established, with herself at its head. She felt a natural affinity for those countries in Europe which had also rejected Catholicism, such as parts of Germany and the Netherlands. The countries that we know today as Holland and Belgium were at that time partly occupied by the Spanish army. In this area, the so-called Spanish Netherlands, Protestantism was not tolerated, the rulers of Spain being devout, not to say fanatical in their Catholic faith. The Spanish Inquisition was of course a byword for religious intolerance. It was not to be wondered at that England offered comfort and support to the Protestants of the Netherlands who were having such a terrible time of it.

Elizabeth's relationship with Spain, and indeed Philip, was complex. At some times, it seemed as though she might be about to marry him, at others, war looked likely. The queen did not want England to go to war with the mightiest empire in the world and preferred to use indirect means to try and reduce the power of Spain. She licensed privateers, which were private ships with a commission to carry out acts of piracy, to operate against Spanish ships carrying gold back to Europe from the mines of South America, while at the same time warning the captains that they must not start a war with Spain. This was what would become known in the twentieth century as 'plausible deniability'. One of these privateers or pirates was Francis Drake.

Today, most people remember Francis Drake as the man who first circumnavigated the globe, travelling all the way round the world by sailing west across the Atlantic from Britain and returning by way of the Indian Ocean and Africa. Drake is often represented as being some kind of famous explorer for undertaking this three-year journey. This monumental voyage was not, though, as many suppose, undertaken in a spirit of adventurous curiosity. It was because having clashed with Spanish ships on the Pacific coast of America, Drake feared that he would be ambushed on the way back to Britain if he attempted to sail around the tip of South America and then back across the Atlantic.

After seizing fabulous quantities of treasure from the Spanish and having good reason to think that the Straits of Magellan, at the tip of South America, would be held against him, Francis Drake headed north and tried to find a way back to Britain by sailing through the Arctic. When this proved impossible, he realized that he would have to go the long way round, by crossing the Pacific Ocean and then sailing past India and round Africa. Exploring did not enter into it – he just wished to get home with all his loot and could not find a quicker way.

By the beginning of 1587, it looked very likely that for one reason or another, either because of the state-licensed piracy endorsed by Queen Elizabeth or the military support being given to Dutch Protestants against the Spanish army occupying part of the Netherlands, England and Spain would probably be at war before long. With the execution in February of that year of the Catholic Mary Queen of Scots, who had a legitimate claim to the throne of England, war looked likely. This was really the last chance for Catholicism returning to England. When, with the approval of Queen Elizabeth, Francis Drake raided the Spanish town of Cadiz in the late Spring and burned many ships which he found there, this likelihood became a racing certainty.

Until the execution of Mary Queen of Scots, Philip II thought that it would be a good scheme if Mary were to take over the throne of England, to which she had a good claim, and then upon her death, his daughter Isabella could become Queen of England. It must be borne in mind that Philip himself had a claim to the throne of England, by virtue of his descent from John of Gaunt, whose son became Henry IV. At any rate, in 1587, he decided that the best solution to his problems with England would be to invade the country and either to set up a puppet government or actually absorb England into his own empire. He therefore made plans for a seaborne invasion fleet of barges to cross the English Channel from the territory which he controlled in what is now Holland and northern France.

Preparations for the Armada or to give it its more formal name, *La felicissima armada*, 'the most fortunate fleet', began in 1587, but its launch was delayed until the following year by Francis Drake's raid on Cadiz in April and May 1587. This exploit became known as 'Singeing the King of Spain's Beard'. Originally, it had been hoped to launch the attack on England in October 1587 and this delay was to have serious implications for the Armada. The whole enterprise seemed to be dogged with misfortune, one way and another, but this did not worry King Philip in the slightest, because he believed that God was behind him and would not let his invasion fail. Because Philip was fighting on behalf of the Catholic faith, he was convinced that his endeavours could not possibly fail. After all, how could God let such a devoted servant's efforts fail to be ultimately crowned with success? This strange and deluded belief must be seen in the context of the Reformation, when some European countries, England among them, were rejecting the authority of the Catholic Church and establishing their own churches, separate from, and not under the authority of, Rome. Little wonder that Pope Sixtus V was an enthusiastic supporter of Philip's plans. The Pope promised those who took part in the invasion of England remission of suffering in purgatory as a reward for their participation in the war against Elizabeth, who was an excommunicated heretic.

King Philip must have been quite sure that God favoured his military enterprise. Why else would he have appointed as its leader Don Alonso de Guzman el Bueno, Duke of Medina Sidonia and Captain-General of Andalusia? Here was a man who wrote frankly to Philip, upon hearing of the task allotted to him, saying, 'My health is not equal to such a voyage, for I know by experience of the little I have been at sea that I am always seasick and always catch cold.' As if this were not enough, the Duke went on to say that, 'Since I have no experience of either the sea, or of war, I cannot feel that I ought to command so important an enterprise.' So horrified were Philip's advisors by this letter, that they made sure that the king never saw it. So it was that in April 1588, Medina Sidonia proceeded to Lisbon, where the great fleet was awaiting its commander. At a service in the city's cathedral on the 25th, he received the standard which he would carry into battle: the arms of Spain, flanked by Jesus and the Madonna. The duke was also given a scroll which bore the motto of the expedition, a quotation from Psalm 74; 'Rise up, o Lord, and vindicate your cause'.

It was plain from his subsequent letters to King Philip, which did actually reach the monarch, that the Duke of Medina Sidonia was more than a little dubious about all this talk of divine approval for the fleet which he had been ordered to command. The Armada began to sail from Lisbon on 9 May, but almost as soon as it had gone to sea freakish storms and high winds blew up; as though the weather were trying to blow them back to port. The mighty Armada, known colloquially as 'La invencible', 'the Invincible', was scattered and dispersed, unable to make headway against raging winds which were absolutely unheard of at that time of year. It was only now that they were at sea that another problem emerged. Many of the provisions, the food and water, had been stored on board since October when the fleet had originally been expected to sail. A lot of it had gone off and even the water was almost undrinkable. The Armada was forced to put in at the northern Spanish port of La Coruna on 19 June to take on fresh food and water.

During the stay in La Coruna, Medina Sidonia again took the opportunity to write to Philip, suggesting that the unseasonable storms might be God's way of hinting that he was not favourably disposed towards the invasion of England. As might have been expected, this idea did not appeal to the king, who replied quite sharply. 'If this were an unjust war, one could indeed take this storm as a sign from our Lord to cease offending him. But being just as it is, one cannot believe that He will disband it.' There was more in the same vein, all to the effect that God was wholeheartedly behind the Armada and guaranteed its success. Philip ended his letter brusquely, by saying that, 'I have dedicated this enterprise to God. Pull yourself together and do your part.' A month after putting in to La Coruna, the Spanish Armada set sail once more for the English Channel and if all went well, Spanish troops would be landing in Kent within a few weeks and then marching on London.

Part of the myth associated with the Spanish Armada is the enormous disparity between the English and Spanish naval forces. It is perfectly true that the Armada was the greatest collection of ships ever seen in Europe, consisting of 130 vessels. The English, by way of comparison, had only 105 ships to confront this great force. This is not the whole picture, however.

The majority of the Spanish ships were merchantmen, which had been adapted to carry troops. Some were merely *urcas*, literally 'hulks', which were only used to carry supplies. Of the 130 ships, only thirty-five or so were warships, designed for fighting at sea. Some of these were galleons, huge floating castles which may have had formidable firepower but were large and unwieldy to manoeuvre. The English had fewer ships, but more of them were actually warships. The English vessels were also lighter and easier to control. They could dodge about and make quick attacks on the slower moving ships of the Armada.

On board the Armada, in addition to the sailors, were 19,000 soldiers who would join the 30,000 Spanish soldiers being assembled in the Netherlands to form the invasion force. The men in the Netherlands, commanded by the Duke of Parma, would cross the Channel in barges under the protection of the Armada. The ship-borne troops would then join them and an army of 50,000 would then move towards London.

We come now to the one thing which most people know about the Spanish Armada; that Francis Drake was playing bowls when it was sighted and refused to take any action until he had finished the game, saying that there was plenty of time to do that and then beat the Spanish afterwards. This incident is an integral part of the myth, for it shows a perfect example of British sangfroid in a crisis. Illustration 8 is of Francis Drake, after he has received news of the Armada and has decided to finish his game of bowls. Surprisingly, for such a neat and satisfying little legend, this story is almost certainly true.

On 29 July, Captain Thomas Fleming was at sea, when caught sight of the Armada as it approached the Lizard Peninsula of Cornwall. He sailed as fast he could to Plymouth, to bring the news to Lord Howard of Effingham, the commander of the English fleet and his deputy, Sir Francis Drake. Fleming apparently found Drake playing bowls in Plymouth and urged him to end his game and prepare to sail to meet the Armada. There would have been little hurry, because the south-west wind which had enable Captain Fleming to race to Plymouth would have worked against launching the English fleet. Not only that, he had come in on the tide, which would not be going out until 10 pm. All things considered, Drake really didn't need to hurry: the ships would be going nowhere for a few hours.

The terrible storms which had already delayed the Armada by a month showed their teeth again as Medina Sidonia came in sight of the Scilly Isles. He wrote of the conditions at sea that, 'It blew a full gale with very heavy rain squalls and the sea was so heavy that all the sailors agreed that they had never seen its equal in July.' Little wonder that Medina Sidonia was beginning to think that the Lord God himself was signalling his displeasure and telling the fleet to turn back. It might, in retrospect, have been better for the duke if he had been able to take the hint.

By dawn of the day following the sighting of the Armada, Lord Howard and his fleet had left Plymouth, with Francis Drake as Vice-Admiral. It can sometimes take more than a grand title to change a man's nature and so it proved with Drake, because brave and swashbuckling as he might have been, he was at heart a pirate, rather than a naval officer. The day after the English set out to shadow the Armada and determine its intentions, the flagship of the Andalusian squadron, the *Nuestra Señora del Rosario*, collided with another ship, the *Santa Catalina*. The *Rosario* suffered serious damage, including breaking her mainmast. With no mainsail, she began to fall behind the rest of the ships. For some reason, Medina Sidonia did not feel inclined to wait for the *Rosario*, even though it was one of the most powerful ships in the fleet. Her commander, Don Pedro de Valdés, was left to fend for himself. The *Rosario* was carrying 50,000 ducats, part of the Armada's pay-chest, a huge fortune. In addition to that, there was also a large quantity of gunpowder and shot. It was a tempting prize, too tempting for one of the former privateers in the English fleet.

When night fell, Francis Drake saw an opportunity to make a little money while in the service of his country. In doing so, he jeopardized not only the fleet of which he was deputy commander, but also the whole of England. His actions on the night of 31 July could have ended with the Spanish invasion and occupation of a large part of Britain, a minor detail of the Spanish Armada myth which is often omitted from history books. Francis Drake had been given the task by Lord Howard of leading the English ships which were following the Armada. His ship, the *Revenge*, had a large poop lantern, which was followed as a guide by the other ships, including Howard's own *Ark Royal*. Without warning, Drake's light was extinguished and the leading English ships were left wondering what had happened. There was nearly a disaster, because the captains of the most important ships, including the flagship *Ark Royal*, the *White Bear* and the *Mary Rose*, caught sight of another light and tried to catch up with it. They proved to be following not Francis Drake, but rather the light of one of the Spanish ships.

The situation could hardly have been more dangerous for the English fleet which was charged with defending the whole country. Unwittingly, their commander-in-chief was separated from his ships and at risk of being surrounded by the Armada. Fortunately, Medina Sidonia did not take advantage of this opportunity and the English were able to fall back and rejoin the fleet. It had been a narrow escape, though, and it turned out to be all Francis Drake's fault. He had been unable to resist the temptation of seizing the *Rosario* and its treasure. This was why he had doused his lantern and slipped off into the night.

Although he later came up with a story about chasing some mysterious ships which he had seen, it was really the *Rosario* and her gold which Drake had been after. Incredibly, Don Pedro, commander of the *Rosario*, surrendered to Francis Drake without a fight, so awed was he by this almost legendary figure. Drake was already well-known to the Spaniards, not least for the attack on Cadiz the previous year. They knew him as 'El Draco', the Dragon. Later trying to justify his decision to yield up his ship without a fight, Don Pedro said of Francis Drake that he was possessed of 'valour and felicity so great that Mars and Neptune seemed to attend him'. Mars was of course the Roman god of war and Neptune the deity of the sea. The Spanish seemed to have been determined to enhance Francis Drake's status as an almost supernatural being who was favoured by strange gods.

This invocation of pagan deities in connection with one of the greatest of English heroes is interesting. The Spanish king believed that the Christian God was on his side and now here was one of his commanders suggesting that other gods appeared to be standing beside the English! All of which served to enhance the mythic nature of Drake's actions against the Spanish Armada. Following its defeat of course, it was widely claimed among Protestants that God was in fact on *their* side and that the unseasonable weather indicated divine support for the Church of England! All this talk of gods, pagan or Christian, ensured that the scattering of the Armada was firmly established in Britain's mythos as a signal instance of how various gods fought on the side of the British Isles against a variety of European nations, whether Spain, France, Holland or Germany.

Not only did Francis Drake's cupidity and greed put the leaders of the English fleet in danger, they also sowed dissension at the very time that it was so vitally important that everybody focused upon warding off the Spanish invasion. Martin Frobisher, another famous privateer, was so incensed by what had happened that he wrote of the way in which Drake had sailed off and kept close to the *Rosario*, lest somebody else should have the treasure she carried, 'Drake's light we looked for but there was no light to be seen. Like a coward he kept by her all night because he would have the spoil.' Although he had been misled as to the true value of the plunder which Drake had seized, there is no doubt that Frobisher knew that he had been cheated out of a considerable sum, which should have been split between others. He wrote that Drake had tried to, 'cozen us of our shares of fifteen thousand ducats'. Finally, the angry captain made it perfectly clear what would happen if he for one didn't get a look in on this prize, 'We will have our shares or I will make him spend the best blood in his belly.' Somehow or other, Lord Howard managed to quieten things down and settle the quarrel between two of his fiercest commanders, but it had been a close thing. Howard could not have been feeling all that well disposed towards Francis Drake himself, for nearly letting his leader be captured by the enemy, just because he was so greedy for gold. This is not at all the image of the famous sailor and explorer which has come down to us today.

Nobody really knew what the aim of the Spanish Armada was. One possibility was that they would try and land troops and take a port on the south coast, Southampton perhaps. Another was that the Spanish might wish to occupy a small part of England and hold it as a base. The Isle of Wight would have made a convenient chunk of England for this purpose. There were lively skirmishes as the two fleets moved up the Channel, with the English ships darting in to attack the larger and slower Spanish vessels. The further the Armada travelled, the more it began to seem as though the only aim was to link up with Parma's forces in the Netherlands, presumably with the intention of landing an invasion force in Kent.

Just as with Hitler's projected invasion of Britain some centuries later, the troops would be carried across the Channel by slow-moving and vulnerable little barges or landing craft and it was essential that these should be protected against enemy attack. In 1940 the efforts of both sides were directed towards securing air superiority, but in 1588 it was of course sea power which would decide the fate of England. The whole purpose of the Armada was to protect the forces being ferried across to Kent from mainland Europe. This could only be achieved if the English ships were kept at bay.

By 6 August, when the Armada had anchored at Calais, there were no more doubts about their precise intention. Unless swift action was taken, England might fall. It was now that the weather, with which the British have for many years enjoyed a love-hate relationship, became a crucial factor in the course of events. The Duke of Parma had not yet begun to embark his troops onto the barges which would take them across the Channel to England; he had been awaiting the arrival of Medina Sidonia and his ships. Time was now working against the English and under Howard and Drake's direction a strategy was devised which, it was hoped, would put the Armada out of commission. The wind was blowing towards Calais and so eight old ships were loaded with barrels of pitch and kegs of gunpowder, which were surrounded with scrap iron to turn them into deadly bombs. On the night of 7 August, these 'hell burners', as they were called, were set on fire and sent sailing towards the Spanish Armada where it lay at anchor.

The blazing ships, from which came at intervals huge explosions which sent shrapnel scything through the men on the Spanish ships, caused panic, as well they might. The Spanish quickly cut their moorings and made into open water to escape the fire-ships. This was what the English fleet had been waiting for and they played havoc with the Armada. After the fierce Battle of Gravelines which ensued, the Spanish were forced to retreat into the North Sea. Only three Spanish ships were actually sunk in the encounter, with no English ships going down, but the weather was worsening rapidly and since the Armada was getting the worst of it and the Channel itself was now securely under the control of the English, there was little to do but go where the wind took them.

The wind, which had already caused so much trouble for the Spanish Armada, was growing stronger, and the sea rougher. Lord Howard pursued the Spanish for four days, until they were somewhere near the Firth of Forth. By that time, the English were running perilously low on provisions and so turned to shore. Storms were still driving the Armada on, the Spanish having no chance of finding a friendly harbour to wait out the poor weather. At some point, Medina Sidonia decided that with the English Channel being held against them, he and his ships would have to return to Spain by going the long way, sailing north, right round Scotland and then into the Atlantic and along the west coast of Ireland, giving Britain as wide a berth as could be managed. It may be argued that he had at this point little choice, but the journey was to prove disastrous.

Nobody could understand what had happened and how their mighty Armada had been so comprehensively defeated by the English. Human nature has not changed over the centuries and just as would be the case today when some military expedition went terribly wrong, there were plenty of people who claimed to have known all along that the invasion was doomed. Medina Sidonia's senior military advisor, Don Francisco de Bobadilla, wrote bitterly about this, as the fleet headed towards Scotland, 'There is nobody aboard this fleet who is not now saying "I told you so" or "I knew this would happen". But it's just like trying to lock the stable door after the horse has bolted.'

We know that the Spanish Armada was defeated, but tend sometimes to give credit for this to Francis Drake and his fellow seadogs. In fact, it was the unexpectedly violent weather for the time of year which brought about the Armada's battering, rather than the guns of the English. It will be recalled that at that famous Battle of Gravelines, only three ships out of the 130 of which the Armada consisted were actually sunk by English cannon fire. The Armada escaped virtually unscathed into the North Sea and despite being harried and pursued by the English, no further vessels were lost to enemy action.

The journey around the coast of the British Isles turned into a nightmare for the Spanish, in which up to a third of their ships were lost. The poor weather continued, driving ships ashore, where the crews were sometimes killed out of hand by Scots and Irishmen who were either fearful of an invasion or desirous of looting wrecks. It was not until late September that the mighty Armada finally limped home to Spain. Even as they approached the shore of Spain, the weather had one last shock in store, as it was struck by the tail-end of an Atlantic hurricane.

Looked at as myth, the story of the Spanish Armada is almost perfect. Not only do we have a legendary warrior, nicknamed 'the Dragon', whom even his enemies suspect has the favour of the gods, we have two rival nations who also believe that they alone are favoured by divine approval. This is a narrative tale of warfare, with strong personalities involved and it is about the salvation of a small nation threatened by a great empire. It was remarked earlier that this is a story which could have been taken from the Bible and there is indeed a kind of Old Testament majesty about the way that a hero, backed by God, is able to sweep his enemies before him. The fierce storms which drove off the Spanish ships put one in mind of the parting of the Red Sea and destruction of Pharaoh's army by the waves. There is a grandeur about this sort of story, which sticks in the mind. This is especially so when you know that it proves that God is on the side of you and your nation! It is for this reason that the downfall of Pharaoh is remembered by the Jews with the same fondness that the British accord to the scattering of the invincible Armada.

The mythologizing of the Spanish Armada began immediately after the Battle of Gravelines and both England and Spain focused upon what the events supposedly told them about the Deity's views and opinions on the Reformation. The authority of the Catholic Church was being challenged in England, Germany, Scandinavia and the Netherlands and one might have thought, as did Philip II, that here was a good opportunity for God to let Europe know where he stood on this question. Was Catholicism the only true religion or might the Lutherans and Anglicans have a point? It was for this very reason that the King of Spain was so confident about the great enterprise. He told those who raised doubts about plans for the invasion of England that because Spain was fighting in God's cause, they could not lose. After the Armada returned, Philip remarked despairingly, 'I sent my ships to fight against men and not the winds and waves of God.'

It was in England and that part of the Netherlands which the Spanish did not occupy that God's actions in the fight against Spain were most clearly seen, which is hardly to be wondered at! In later years, the phrase, 'the Protestant wind', was widely used in reference to the storms which delayed and then caused so much harm to the Armada. Queen Elizabeth was responsible for a great deal of this. She even wrote a song of thanksgiving about the victory, similar in many ways to the Biblical Song of Miriam after Pharaoh's army had been vanquished by the sea. Elizabeth wrote that, 'He made the winds and the water rise, to scatter all mine enemies.' She went on modestly to call herself the 'handmaid' of the Lord.

The Biblical theme of the battle between those whom God favours and those he wishes to destroy was continued when commemorative medals were issued in both England and the free part of the Netherlands which also emphasized the role that God had taken against the Spanish forces. These medals bore the inscription, 'He blew with His winds and they were scattered'. The 'He' in this context being of course the Lord. This was based upon another Biblical quotation, this time from the book of Job. Chapter 4, Verse 9 says, 'By the blast of God they perish, and by the breath of his nostrils they are consumed.' Now the myth was taking an even more impressive form. God had not only stirred up the waters to disrupt the efforts of Spain, he had actually blown at the ships himself to sink them. There could be little doubt after this how the Lord of Heaven and Earth felt about Protestantism in general and the British Isles in particular. There were clearly very dear to his heart!

The significance of the Battle of Gravelines and the rout of the Armada was very great, not only for Britain but also for the rest of the world. At that time, the Spanish were the masters of the New World, which is to say North and South America, but now things began to change. England was becoming a naval force to be reckoned with and so North America became a Protestant area, settled by people from western, rather than southern, Europe. Those storms in the English Channel and North Sea were of world-historical importance and ultimately shaped North America into the form it takes today. The United States, the world's only superpower, has its roots in those events of 1588.

Myth in history serves a number of purposes, one of which is to simplify and help us to make sense of masses of information and facts. It provides a framework, so that we can see certain threads and compare one type of episode to another. This is why the defeat of the Spanish Armada was likened to the drowning in the sea of Pharaoh's army. These were both examples of God intervening in human affairs and showing whose side he was on. Myth of this sort helps us to select salient facts and see patterns in the past. This explains in part why we talk of 1588 as being the year of '*the* Spanish Armada' and not '*a* Spanish Armada' or 'the *first* Spanish Armada'. The Armada of 1588 was dealt with so neatly, by a combination of British pluck and divine aid, that it would spoil the narrative were we to realize that there were actually a succession of the things over the course of a decade or so. Besides, those later Armadas didn't feature the larger-than-life figure of Francis Drake, the famous hero who was the first man to circumnavigate the world. Those other Armadas would just muddle everything up. More than that, looking at later incidents in the war with Spain might make us question the idea that our brave sailors were always on hand to protect Britain during the Elizabethan Era and prevent enemies landing on our shores.

This is probably why we tend to gloss over historical incidents such as the Battle of Cornwall, which took place in 1595: they do not fit in with our image of indomitable Tudor England, a country not to be trifled with. We have a vague idea that there was no successful foreign invasion of English soil after the Norman Conquest, but of course this is not really true. On 2 August 1595 four Spanish galleys arrived off the coast of Cornwall. They were the *Nuestra Señora de Begona, Salvador, Peregrina* and *Bazana* and on board were three companies of men armed with matchlock muskets, about 400 soldiers in total.

Since the days of the first Spanish Armada, England was supposed to be ready for any attack from hostile ships, but the militia in the region of Mount's Bay fled at the sight of the heavily-armed Spanish troops. Before landing their forces, the galleys bombarded Penzance with their cannons, destroying hundreds of homes. After the Spaniards landed, they spent two days burning and looting. Penzance was put to the torch, along with the villages of Mousehole, Paul and Newlyn. Only a dozen or so men, led by the Deputy Lord-Lieutenant of the county, opposed this little invasion, but to no avail. After burning down a few towns, the Spanish stole the very cannons from the local fort and rowed them out to their ships! A fleet commanded by Francis Drake and John Hawkins, another famous Elizabethan seadog, was unable either to prevent this temporary occupation of English soil, nor to catch those responsible once they put to sea again. One quite sees why this is not the sort of story which might enhance the myth of Sir Francis Drake and his nautical prowess.

The second Spanish Armada was launched in the autumn of 1596 and while not quite as big as the first one, still consisted of scores of heavily-armed warships carrying thousands of troops, including 3,000 cavalry. Just like the first Armada, the weather came to England's assistance and struck this second fleet before it even came within sight of Britain. A third Armada was assembled the following year and the intention was once again to land in Cornwall and hold it as a Spanish base. As with the previous two Armadas, storms wrecked this invasion force and it achieved nothing.

The Battle of Cornwall is the most significant of the Spanish incursions into English waters during the late sixteenth century. Significant in that it was the longest occupation of territory, but also because it has been almost entirely forgotten today. The attack on Cadiz undertaken by Francis Drake, which became known as the 'Singeing of the King of Spain's Beard', has come down to us over the centuries and ties in with the sort of daring exploits which we expect of the bold buccaneer. That the Spanish not only bombarded Penzance but landed and held the area for two days is all but unknown to anybody other than historians specializing in the period.

Today, we are less apt to attribute military success to divine agency and so the belief that God came to the aid of England at a particularly tricky time for the nation is not one to which many people would now subscribe. Most of us are, however, quite happy to buy in to the myth of the daring and valiant leader of men who took on the might of the greatest empire the world had known at that time and humble it. Singeing the King of Spain's beard, indeed; what a guy! Whenever talk turns to creating a new Bank Holiday in Britain, there are always suggestions that we adopt 8 August, to commemorate the defeat of the Armada by Francis Drake.

What did Drake actually achieve during those summer days in 1588? The answer is, when all the glamour and exaggeration is stripped away, precious little. The first thing to bear in mind is that famous as he was, Francis Drake was not in charge of the fleet which tackled the Armada. That distinction went to Lord Howard of Effingham. Strangely enough, while everybody has heard of Francis Drake, Howard is all but unknown. Apart from nearly scuppering the defence of England by causing the commander-in-chief to be captured by the enemy, Drake's role was really limited to firing ineffectually at the ships of the Armada. Just how ineffectual this cannonade was may judged by the fact that for a week the English fleet followed the Spanish

Armada from Devon to Calais, firing all the way, until they were almost out of powder. Not one Spanish ship was sunk by this constant activity. Even when their fireships had lured the enemy out into combat, the combined efforts of the English ships only resulted in the loss of three ships of the Armada, which is singularly unimpressive.

What really drove the Armada away from the projected landing site in Kent was not the English fleet, but rather the prevailing winds. Even this random meteorological phenomenon was enlisted in support of the mythic narrative which grew up around the defeat of the Armada, with God Himself being given a role in the drama. Perhaps it was this combination of the larger-than-life, swashbuckling Francis Drake with his cannons blazing, assisted by the breath of the Deity, which cemented the Spanish Armada in the British psyche.

Chapter 4

Mutiny on the *Bounty* 1789:
'I have been in hell for weeks with you.'

It may at first sight seem strange to include the story of the mutiny on the *Bounty* in a collection of myths which shaped Britain. Surely this was a fairly trivial incident, which might be of some interest as an historical curiosity, but has no wider significance? The tale of Captain Bligh and the conflict between him and Fletcher Christian is of interest because it is a variation of the 'little man against authority' mythic narrative. In this case, it shows a young idealist struggling against an older, conventional leader in a position of power over him. Everybody reading the story of the mutiny which took place on that ship of the Royal Navy in the late eighteenth century feels an instinctive sympathy for Christian and the other mutineers. After all, we know what a dreadful place the navy was at that time, with its ferocious discipline and savage punishments like flogging and keel-hauling. Who can blame the sensitive young officer for rebelling on behalf of the suffering sailors and going off to seek a peaceful Pacific island where they could all live in harmony? Besides which, we have all been young ourselves and most of us know what it is like, either in a job, school or family, to clash with the generation above us, whose ideas are hidebound and reactionary. More people can more readily identify with Fletcher Christian than they can the notorious Captain Bligh, and it is this which gives this story its special interest and has led to the making of five dramatic films, all of them colourful and wholly misleading accounts of the mutiny.

The story of Christian and Bligh had a great impact at the time, chiefly due to the times in which it occurred. The mutiny took place in April 1789, the year that the French Revolution began. Just three months after Bligh and other loyal members of his crew were cast adrift in an open boat, the Bastille was stormed in Paris. One of the first act of the mutineers from the *Bounty*, once they had deposed the commander of the ship and set him adrift in an open boat, was to make new clothes from an old sail, clothes which meant that they were all equal and that bore no badges of rank.

By the time that the mutineers were brought to trial, three years later, Europe was fascinated by the whole idea of idealism leading to rebellion against the established order. In a sense, the actual causes of the quarrel between William Bligh and Fletcher Christian were irrelevant; it was what the two men stood for that counted. Little wonder that Romantic poets such as William Wordsworth declared their support on behalf of the young man who had risen in protest and overthrown the captain of the ship in which he had been sailing – it tied in perfectly with the spirit of the times. Everywhere one looked, the image of small men seeking a better life for themselves than that afforded by conventional society as it was currently ordered in Europe could be seen. There were echoes too of the American Revolution in the affair. Had it occurred in 1689 or 1889, it is most unlikely that we would find this incident of any great interest.

The clash of youthful idealism with the old, established order, that we see in the mutiny on the *Bounty*, has a curious resonance with the subject of our next chapter, which is the Battle of Waterloo. Although, ostensibly at least, the famous military engagement in Belgium bears no points of similarity with the rebellion on a Royal Navy ship over twenty-five years earlier, the underlying theme is in fact identical. Napoleon too represented new ideas, championed by a young man, which shook the established order in Europe and precipitated the period known as the Napoleonic Wars. The Duke of Wellington, by contrast, symbolized the old traditions, opposing change and championing the status quo. Waterloo settled the matter, at least in Europe, in favour of the conservatives against the radicals and revolutionaries.

We have so far looked at three episodes from British history and found that the versions we learned at school are greatly at variance with the facts, as far as they can be reliably established. In the case of the mutiny on HMS *Bounty*, we will discover that almost no part of the story as it is currently understood is even remotely true. Captain Bligh's name has become a byword for tyranny and the exercise of cruel authority over helpless men and yet, according to the official records, he was one of the most lenient captains in the whole of the British Navy! At a time when floggings were ordered on board ships for the most trifling of reasons, Bligh was responsible for fewer floggings than any other ship's commander. The friction between him and his crew stemmed more from Bligh's compassionate nature and desire to maintain his crew's health than because he was given to excessive punishment. Before looking in detail at William Bligh though, perhaps we should see how he and Fletcher Christian came to be on the ill-fated *Bounty* in the first place.

Before we go any further, I wonder if any alert readers have spotted the deliberate mistakes above, when referring to William Bligh? Bligh is almost universally called 'Captain' Bligh in accounts of the mutiny and I followed this convention above, but in fact he was nothing of the sort; his rank was that of lieutenant. Lieutenant Bligh does not emphasize the power of the man though, when we are looking at the mutiny as a clash between youthful impetuosity and established order and so he has become 'Captain' Bligh. It is true that as the senior officer in charge of the vessel, Bligh would have been addressed as 'captain' by the crew, while at sea, but this was merely a customary courtesy among sailors. Nobody in 1789 would have referred to him as 'Captain Bligh', because of course he was really Lieutenant Bligh. It would not be until several years after the mutiny on the *Bounty* that William Bligh would be promoted to the rank of captain. Because 'Captain' is a title redolent of authority, it fits better with the mythic theme of young revolutionaries defying their elders and allows William Bligh to stand in as a proxy for all the officers whom those men were determined to defy. Illustration 9 shows a blue plaque on the house where Bligh lived and refers to him more correctly as the 'commander' of the *Bounty*, rather than 'captain'.

When the *Bounty* left England in the winter of 1787, the slave trade was in full swing, with the economies of the Caribbean islands being almost wholly dependent upon forced labour. Obviously, the more cheaply that one is able to house and feed slaves, the higher the profit margin on their labour. It is perfectly possible to maintain health and vitality on a pretty restricted diet, as was seen in Ireland, at the time when the staple diet of most of the population consisted almost entirely of potatoes. It was suggested that a plant found growing wild in the South Pacific might enable the plantation owners of the Caribbean to feed their slaves cheaply. The plant in question was the breadfruit tree, which is related to the mulberry.

Breadfruit is a starchy fruit which tastes something like potatoes and is very rich in Vitamin C. If Irish peasants were able to subsist entirely on potatoes, so went the reasoning, might it be possible to feed the slaves in colonies like Jamaica primarily on breadfruit? The task of the *Bounty* was to sail to the island of Tahiti, in the Pacific, cultivate a thousand breadfruit plants there and then transport them all the way to the West Indies. Put like that, the enterprise sounds absurdly easy, just another routine sea voyage by sailors of the Royal Navy. What went wrong and turned this expedition into one of the most famous nautical incidents of the eighteenth century? More people today can name Bligh's ship than are able offhand to say what Captain Cook's ship, in which he discovered Australia, was called. This is a strange state of affairs, in that the colonization of Australia was of enormous historical importance, whereas the mutiny which took place in the Pacific

20 years later was a trifling matter. That the *Bounty* became known to every-body, while the *Endeavour* has become an obscure footnote, unfamiliar to anybody other than those with a particular interest in the period, tells us that something other than a mutiny was involved and that the affair of the *Bounty* stirs images and ideas in us in a way that the mere discovery of a new continent can never do.

The *Bounty* had been partly converted into a greenhouse or nursery for young plants, before even setting sail. A glazed and drained area, ordinarily the Great Cabin on a ship of that sort, was constructed so that the thousand breadfruit plants could be carried safely from the Pacific to the Caribbean. This made conditions on board cramped from the very beginning and may have contributed to the ill-feeling which led eventually to mutiny.

Lieutenant William Bligh was put in command of the *Bounty* and chose Fletcher Christian, with whom he had already served, to be the Master. In the event, another man was given this post, leaving Christian as Master's Mate. Bligh and Christian had a master-pupil relationship, Bligh being a little over ten years older than the 23-year-old Christian. The two men had socialized together and this was to make Bligh all the more incredulous when the mutiny broke out.

When the *Bounty* set sail on 23 December 1787, the intention was that she would sail across the Atlantic and then pass Cape Horn on the south-ern tip of South America and so enter the Pacific Ocean and make her way to Tahiti to pick up the breadfruit plants. In early April 1788, the *Bounty* reached Cape Horn, but was unable to round it because of the fierce storms and mountainous waves. After spending two weeks waiting for conditions to improve, the decision was made to sail back across the Atlantic and the head south and enter the Indian Ocean, making their way into the Pacific from there. This long diversion probably did little for anybody's good spir-its. Tahiti was not reached until October, by which time the *Bounty* had travelled over 30,000 miles.

Relations between William Bligh and his protégé were, at first, warm. Bligh treated Christian as though he were his assistant and even lent him money. There was no warning of what was to come. Despite the reputation which Bligh acquired after the mutiny for being a strict disciplinarian, he was in fact one of the most relaxed and humane officers in the Royal Navy. His only real fault was that he had an exceedingly sharp tongue and was apt to use it at the least excuse. But at a time when floggings and hangings were far from uncommon occurrences on British ships, Bligh went out of his way not to impose any punishment at all unless it was strictly necessary. After having to order twelve lashes for Matthew Quintal for, 'insolence and muti-nous behaviour', Bligh recorded in the log book that, 'Until this afternoon I had hoped that I could have performed the voyage without punishment to anyone.' In Tahiti, three sailors deserted, taking with them muskets and powder. When they were captured a few weeks later, Bligh would have been acting perfectly correctly had he had them court-martialled and hanged. As it was, he simply had them flogged, which was an act of great leniency.

When he was in his early twenties, William Bligh had sailed with Captain Cook and acquired from him an almost fanatical dedication to hygiene and cleanliness. He was determined to keep the ship and the men on it clean and healthy. To this end, he insisted on regular dancing in the evenings, for healthy exercise, as well as the consumption of vegetables to ward off the deficiency diseases such as scurvy which were so rife on ships at that time. For all that these measures might have been designed with the best interests of his men at heart, they did not serve to make Bligh popular with some of the sailors on the *Bounty*. They felt, with some justification, that their captain was treating them more like fractious children than grown men. This was indeed Bligh's view of the case. He wrote once that, 'Seamen will seldom attend to themselves, they must be watched like children.' In addition to insisting that they kept their quarters clean and ate up their greens, Bligh also made sure that the men under his command got plenty of sleep. The tradition was at that time on ships of the Royal Navy that men were on duty four hours out of eight. Bligh altered this to four hours in twelve, which was a distinct improvement.

There seems little enough during the voyage to Tahiti of which any reasonable seaman of the time might complain. Their captain was a paternalistic man who assumed that those under his command were not really capable of taking care of themselves, but this was surely an irritation, rather than a cause to risk one's neck in taking part in a mutiny. The penalties for such an action were severe indeed and any man who raised his hand against the captain might expect to be hanged for it. There was in reality none of the starvation and savage floggings which have been so luridly depicted in the Hollywood films made about the voyage. Perhaps comparing one of those films with the reality might underline this point.

Here is Clark Gable, playing the part of Fletcher Christian in the 1935 version of *Mutiny on the Bounty*. He is accusing Bligh, played by Charles Laughton, of mistreating the crew

The captains I've served with before didn't starve their men. They didn't save money by buying up the stinking meat. They didn't buy

yams that would sicken a pig. They didn't call their men thieves and
flog them to the bone ...

This then is the traditional view of 'Captain' Bligh; a vicious martinet, whose
crew suffered dreadfully under his rule. We shall examine this charge-sheet
later and see upon what Hollywood based their partisan view of the case.
This is necessary, for it is the image of William Bligh and Fletcher Christian
which is generally held to this day.

It was in Tahiti that the seeds of mutiny were really sown. Because of
their delay in arriving – it took almost a year to get to the island – the *Bounty*
arrived at the start of the rainy season. This meant that it was necessary to
stay anchored there for the next five months so that the breadfruit plants
could be cultivated in readiness for the long journey to the West Indies.
During that time, Bligh was quite relaxed about the fact that his crew were
spending their free time ashore and forming liaisons with various women
living on the island. After their long and arduous journey, Tahiti must have
seemed like paradise to the sailors, a view, incidentally, that Bligh himself
shared. He wrote in his log that the island was

> Certainly the paradise of the world, and if happiness could result
> from situation and convenience, here it is to be found in the highest
> perfection. I have seen many parts of the world, but Otaheite is
> capable of being preferable to them all.

Although he did not take a native lover himself, there is every reason to suppose that Bligh was tolerant about this happening among the crew, as long as
the breadfruit were cultivated and the ship kept ready to sail when the rainy
season came to an end.

In January, almost three months after the *Bounty* arrived in Tahiti,
came the first serious problem. There had been friction and disagreements
between the captain and his crew during the voyage, but these all blew over
fairly quickly. Although Bligh had a hot temper and was prone to exploding in fury at some fancied offence, his anger was manifested only in sharp
words. As soon as the matter was ended, he seemed to forget all about it and
expect others to do the same. When three of the crew went missing along
with a considerable quantity of arms and ammunition, however, this had
to be dealt with firmly. The men concerned were Charles Churchill, John
Millward and William Muspratt. They had had enough of being under naval
discipline and hoped to disappear on Tahiti until the *Bounty* had left and

simply carry on living with their Polynesian lovers in what they too saw as some kind of Garden of Eden.

When the deserters were tracked down and brought back to the ship, Bligh had two choices. He could, had he been so minded, have brought them to court-martial on a charge of deserting and stealing weapons. Since the *Bounty* was on active service, the Articles of War applied and there could be little doubt that the men would have been found guilty and hanged. Instead, the captain chose to address the matter informally, having the men flogged and placed in irons. It is recorded that the three of them were very grateful for this mercy and knew that they had got off lightly and escaped with their lives. It is upon this incident, which actually earned the gratitude of the supposed 'victims', that the idea of Bligh being a ferocious disciplinarian is founded. It has already been remarked that there were fewer floggings on the *Bounty* than on any other Royal Navy ship operating in the Pacific.

When the time was up and the *Bounty* made ready to leave Tahiti, on the afternoon of 5 April 1789, many of the sailors probably felt regret at leaving this beautiful place and were far from enchanted at the idea of sailing to the other side of the world to deliver a load of potted plants to islands in the Caribbean. It is likely that very few of the men on the *Bounty* felt very cheerful about life.

This kind of thing, though, was the lot of the British sailor and mutiny was a very rare thing in the Royal Navy. It is almost certainly the case that it was less that William Bligh was a cruel tyrant than that he had a very emotional and unstable second-in-command which brought about the rebellion which ended in the ship's commander being set adrift in an open boat.

Fletcher Christian came from what would then have been termed a 'good family', meaning one which was well-educated, well-to-do and well-connected. His brother Edward was a professor of law at Cambridge University, a fact that was to have some bearing on the creation of the myth of the mutiny on the *Bounty*. The captain treated the young man as his assistant and representative. This was not an unalloyed pleasure for a sensitive man like Christian, because being close to Bligh meant bearing the brunt of the older man's anger and being on the receiving end of tongue-lashings, which apparently really upset Christian. After one particular episode, a member of the crew testified that Fletcher Christian had tears running down his face at the mortification of being publicly upbraided in so harsh a fashion.

It is altogether possible that it took the crew of the *Bounty* a little while to adjust to naval discipline after their sojourn on Tahiti. William Bligh, as we have seen, regarded the sailors under his command as being little better than children, who had to be constantly scolded in order to get them to do things properly. Three weeks after leaving Tahiti, matters came to a head.

There was increasing personal tension between Bligh and Christian. This was no secret; indeed, on a small ship of that sort, it would hardly have been possible for others not to hear their captain abusing the younger man. On the night of 21 April, Christian was overheard saying to the captain, 'Sir, your abuse is so bad that I cannot do my duty with any pleasure. I have been in hell for weeks with you.'

On 22 April, the *Bounty* anchored off the most inaptly named Friendly Islands, now known as Tonga. The aim was to collect supplied of water and wood for the next leg of their journey. Fletcher Christian was put in charge of the boat sent to shore. Anxious to avoid bloodshed and confrontation with the inhabitants of the islands, Bligh allowed muskets to be taken in the boat, but ordered Christian to leave them in the boat when he and his men landed and not to carry them about when they were collecting the provisions. When there was trouble with the islanders and Christian was obliged to leave in a hurry, Bligh was furious and called him, 'a damned cowardly rascal'. For a young man of good family to be spoken to in this way in front of everybody was unusual, but William Bligh made no allowances for status or class. He spoke to his second-in-command just as he would to any other seaman whom he suspected of dereliction of duty. It is worth remembering here that the expression 'damned', while considered today the very mildest of expletives was, 200 years ago, among the strongest of words that might be used in an argument. As late as the 1930s, there was great debate when making the film of *Gone With the Wind*, as to whether it would be possible to include the word 'damn' in what was meant to be a family entertainment. For Bligh to curse one of his officers in such terms was really a bit much.

The ill-feeling which led to the mutiny was essentially a personal matter between the bitterly resentful Fletcher Christian and his hot-tempered commander. A journal kept by the boatswain's mate, James Morrison, suggests strongly that after leaving Tahiti, there was no thought of mutiny in anybody's mind. He noted, though, that Bligh was even more irritable than usual and that he spoke very sharply to Fletcher Christian. Matters came to a head when Bligh accused Christian of knowing about the apparent theft of some coconuts. A pile of coconuts had been left on the deck of the *Bounty* and Bligh got it into his head that people had been helping themselves to them, which would not have been in the least surprising. After questioning various other men, he chose to lay the blame on Fletcher Christian. After hinting in this way, Christian asked outright what the captain was driving at, saying, 'I hope you don't think me guilty of stealing?'

James Morrison wrote down an account of this whole affair at the time and it is from his journal and the later evidence given at the courts martial of some of the mutineers that we know what led to the mutiny. Bligh replied to Christian's question by saying 'Yes, you damned hound, I do. You must have stolen them from me or you could give a better account of them.' After this angry exchange, Bligh calmed down and invited Christian to dine with him that evening, as he often did. Fletcher Christian was left with tears, 'running fast from his eyes in big drops'.

Just before the sun rose the next day, Fletcher Christian and several other men burst into Bligh's cabin and forced him from his bed. His hands were tied behind his back and he was led out onto the deck. Christian announced that he was taking over the ship and that the captain was to be set adrift in one of the small boats carried on the *Bounty*. It is now that the myth of this mutiny as a popular uprising against a cruel and inhumane officer really breaks down in the most spectacular way possible, because more than half the ship's crew wished to join Bligh in the boat, rather than remain on the *Bounty* with Christian and the men he was leading. This was in spite of the fact that to undertake a long voyage in the tiny craft must have seemed tantamount to a death sentence. Over twenty of the crew still preferred to remain loyal to their captain. So many wished to throw in their lot with Bligh, that there was not room enough for them all in the boat. They begged Bligh to remember that they had chosen to follow him and not Christian, to which he replied, 'Never fear, my lads. I'll do you justice if I ever reach England.'

The plight of the nineteen men in the 23-foot long launch was perilous in the extreme. Although they had been given water, bread and a compass, they were many miles from the nearest land. All that they could do was rely upon William Bligh's skill as a navigator to save them. The twenty-five men who remained on the *Bounty* turned the ship around and headed back to Tahiti.

Bligh might have been a tough and outspoken man, with a knack for rubbing others up the wrong way, but in a desperate situation such as this, he came into his own. It was his iron discipline during the next two months which saved the lives of those who had chosen to stay with their captain. Conditions in the boat were dreadful, with no shelter at all and barely enough water and food to keep the men alive. Bligh rationed out the water at a quarter of a pint a day and weighed out the bread in two-ounce measures. This meagre diet was supplemented by the catching of fish and the occasional seabird. There were violent thunderstorms, which meant that the men had to bale out frantically, to avoid their fragile vessel sinking. Most became ill and suffered from exposure, but William Bligh somehow maintained their spirits, even organizing sing-songs!

The nearest European settlement was in the Dutch East Indies, some 4,000 miles from the point in the Pacific where they had been cast adrift. Never the less, on 14 June 1790. Bligh's boat arrived at Timor and his crew were saved. It took him the best part of a year in total after the mutiny to get back to England. When he did so, the Royal Navy determined at once to scour the Pacific Ocean for the men who had taken part in the mutiny.

Fletcher Christian and the others had not had an easy time of it. Once rid of their captain, they had thrown all the breadfruit plants into the sea and made themselves new uniforms, without any badges of rank. This was to symbolize the fact that all of them were now equal. The ideas of the American and French Revolutions were clearly at work, at least in the educated mind of Christian, who was the driving force behind all that happened. When the navy came looking for the men, two years later, they found some on Tahiti, but there was no trace of Christian. He and some of the others, along with a number of Tahitian men and women had settled on Pitcairn Island, where they set up what amounted to a colony. In fighting over women, Christian and some of the other mutineers were killed by the Tahitians, who were then murdered themselves. After a time, things settled down and the community became a peaceful one.

Up to this point, there is nothing especially remarkable about the events on the *Bounty*. Mutinies were uncommon in the British navy, but they did happen from time to time and there was no reason to see this as any different from the other cases where a crew had seized control of a ship. However, the *Bounty* had happened to sail at a time of great upheaval throughout Europe and North America, and partly due to this it was destined for immortality of a kind. Before seeing how this occurred, we might look back to the quotation from 'Fletcher Christian' in the 1935 film;

> The captains I've served with before didn't starve their men. They didn't save money by buying up the stinking meat. They didn't buy yams that would sicken a pig. They didn't call their men thieves and flog them to the bone...

Flogging men 'to the bone' refers to the three deserters whose lives Bligh spared. The captain didn't starve his men, merely threatened to reduce their ration of yams. The food on the *Bounty* was good and, as we saw earlier,

Bligh was very concerned about his crew's dietary requirements. The only true bit of this speech is that Christian was actually called a thief, but shortly afterwards Bligh invited him to dine as usual and it is reasonable to suppose that this was just an outburst of temper.

Nothing so far really supports the accepted status of 'Captain' Bligh as a tyrannical slave-driver and it was not until the courts martial of the surviving mutineers that this notion emerged. The ten men were all tried together at Portsmouth on 12 September 1792. The legal situation could hardly have been more clear-cut. When a mutiny takes place on a ship, there can be no such thing as a neutral bystander. Every member of the crew has a duty to help the captain put down any mutiny and simply refusing to help one side or the other makes one every bit as guilty of mutiny as those actually taking arms against authority. The Articles of War, under which the *Bounty* was sailing, were very plain, Article XIX stating that:

> If any person in or belonging to the Fleet shall make or endeavour to make any mutinous Assembly upon any Pretence whatsoever, every Person offending herein, and being convicted thereof by the Sentence of the Court-martial shall suffer Death.

Of the ten men on trial, four were acquitted and six convicted and sentenced to death by hanging. Three of these men were pardoned and at the end of October just three of the *Bounty* mutineers were hanged from the yard-arm of HMS *Brunswick*. The matter was closed and there was no reason to think that there was anything out of the ordinary about the case. Needless to say, as leader of the mutiny, Fletcher Christian was largely held to blame for what had happened and both prosecution and defence did their best to lay on the absent man's shoulders the full responsibility for what had happened in the Pacific on that fateful April day. There was also a good deal of blackguarding of the character of another man who was not present at the court martial. William Bligh had been despatched by the Admiralty on another expedition to the Pacific to collect breadfruit plants and so it was safe for the defendants to make various allegations about his conduct during the earlier voyage.

After the court martial was over, the attorney for one of those convicted but later pardoned for his part in the mutiny published the minutes of the trial. This was done at the urging of Edward Christian who, it will be recalled, was Fletcher Christian's brother and a well-known jurist. He contributed an appendix to the minutes of the court martial, in which he blamed William Bligh's conduct for provoking the mutiny in the first place.

Until the publication of the minutes and their appendix, the only account of the events of the *Bounty*'s voyage had been those written by Bligh in *A Narrative of the Mutiny on the Bounty* and also *A Voyage to the South Sea*.

Every so often, there are affairs in Britain which capture the imagination of the public and cause sides to be taken. Usually these things are trifling matters which are soon forgotten but sometimes, due to the circumstances prevailing, they assume a symbolic importance. So it was with the mutiny on the *Bounty*. Everywhere one looked in the late 1780s and early 1790s, there were signs of revolutionary change in the air. Britain's colony in America had been lost to revolution, France had fallen in the same way and there were stirrings in Britain as many ordinary people became dissatisfied with the political and social situation as it was at that time. Captain Bligh, as he was universally known, represented the established order, rigid, dictatorial and tyrannical. Young Fletcher Christian, on the other hand, was a symbol of youthful rebellion, a man who wished only to live an unrestricted life with his fellows in an earthly paradise. There was certainly something attractive about this idea. Nobody, not even his own brother, denied that Christian had led a revolt, but was he perhaps justified in doing so?

Edward Christian's appendix to the minutes of the courts martial of the mutineers from the *Bounty* was one strand in the birth of the myth of the mutiny on the *Bounty*, but another came from a most surprising direction. Fletcher Christian had grown up in the Lake District town of Cockermouth. A childhood acquaintance of his was one William Wordsworth, who of course went on to become one of the most famous English poets of all time. Wordsworth and his contemporary, Samuel Taylor Coleridge, were leading members of the Romantic Movement and the story of Fletcher Christian exercised a strange fascination for them. It was the idea of those young sailors throwing off the shackles of the harsh discipline of the Royal Navy and wishing to live a free life beneath palm trees on a tropical island which fitted perfectly the notions of such poets and artists.

Not only did Wordsworth and Coleridge champion the mutineers of the *Bounty*, it is possible that they actually saw Christian after his supposed death and, even more peculiarly, might have commemorated the mutiny in two of their most well-known literary works! When the rumour became current that far from being killed on a Pacific island, Fletcher Christian had actually returned to England and was living in Devon, a pamphlet was published containing letters which had supposedly been written by Christian. Wordsworth wrote to the newspapers, saying that he, 'had it on the best authority' that these letters were forgeries. Some assumed that by the 'best authority', William Wordsworth was hinting that Fletcher Christian was indeed in England and that Wordsworth had been in touch with him.

The day after Wordsworth wrote to the *Weekly Entertainer*, denouncing the spurious letters, his sister Dorothy wrote that he was composing a tragedy. In fact, this was to be the only play which William Wordsworth wrote and it was called *The Borderers*. The plot involved a mutiny and a man being thrown off a ship and abandoned on a deserted island. Some saw in this an echo of the mutiny on the *Bounty*.

Wordsworth's inclusion of a mutiny in his literary work, just as he was writing to a newspaper about Fletcher Christian, may have been a coincidence. His neighbour and fellow Romantic poet, Samuel Taylor Coleridge, was also working on perhaps his most famous poem at this time and that too had a curious resonance with the affair of the *Bounty*. In that instance, it was probably not a coincidence that the poem was set largely on board a ship, because in a notebook which he was keeping at the time, Coleridge had written, 'Adventures of Christian, the mutineer'.

In *The Rime of the Ancient Mariner* the eponymous hero is on board a ship when he commits a terrible crime, as a result of which, all his shipmates die. At the end of the poem, the mariner returns to his own country and finds absolution. It has been supposed by some critics that this ending is a coded reference to Fletcher Christian's return to Britain after the mutiny which he instigated.

It was, among other things, the interest shown by poets such as Wordsworth and Coleridge which created and maintained sympathy for Fletcher Christian and the other men who had mutinied on the *Bounty*. Christian is an early archetype of the little man rebelling against authority, a popular figure in British mythology. He also represents at this time the young idealist struggling against the established order and as such, he ties in neatly with the next chapter, which concerns the final battle between the Emperor Napoleon and the Duke of Wellington.

Chapter 5

The Battle of Waterloo 1815:
'The nearest run thing you ever saw in your life'

There may be doubts about the facts surrounding the mutiny on the *Bounty*, but we come now to an integral part of the nation's history about which there can surely be no possible dispute; that Britain won the Battle of Waterloo. Even asking the very question, 'Did Britain win the Battle of Waterloo?' sounds absurd. After all, if we didn't win it, who did? It is a very curious thing that it is in general only in books published in Britain that the Duke of Wellington and the British army are credited with having defeated Napoleon at the last battle which he ever fought, which took place in Belgium on 18 June 1815. It is not a view that one will often find advanced in books produced in other European countries. In Germany, for example, they have quite a different view as to who was responsible for beating Napoleon in 1815. How is this possible?

The standard narrative of Wellington and the Battle of Waterloo is simple and straightforward. It is a classic and enduring instance of the mythic narrative of the British army crossing the Channel and sorting out Europe's problems for her. Napoleon was a dictator who was determined to bring the whole of Europe under his control by means of armed conflict, installing in the process puppet rulers in countries such as Italy, men who would do his bidding. This tyrant then attempted to bring Britain to heel by the institution of a blockade intended to strangle British trade with Europe, which was known as the Continental System. Eventually, Britain had had enough and, partly to defend her own interests but also for the good of the whole Continent, set out to oppose and ultimately depose the Emperor of France. The British and their allies succeeded in doing so in 1814. Napoleon was exiled to the Mediterranean island of Elba. A year later, he escaped, gathered a mighty army and once again faced Britain on the battlefield, near the obscure Belgian village of Waterloo. There, the British commander Wellington inflicted a crushing defeat upon Napoleon and he was exiled once more, this time to Saint Helena, a remote island in the South Atlantic, where he died a few years later.

This then is how the story is taught in British schools and how most educated people in Britain today understand the background to and final resolution of the Battle of Waterloo. How is this major incident in European history viewed on the other side of the English Channel? To begin with, the hero of Waterloo, the general who vanquished Napoleon Bonaparte, is not Wellington, but rather a man of whom hardly anybody in Britain is likely to have heard. His name was Gebhard Leberecht von Blücher, Fürst von Wahlstatt, and he was a Prussian soldier. He may be seen in Illustration 11. It is at this point that we recall something which is seldom mentioned in Britain when the subject of Waterloo comes up, that only a fifth of the soldiers fighting against the French that day were British. The overwhelming majority were German. The Battle of Waterloo as a German victory! This, for those brought up in Britain, is a disconcerting thought indeed.

We shall see shortly that most of the salient facts about the Battle of Waterloo, including the real reason for Napoleon's defeat, are quite unknown today. Not that this really matters, for Waterloo has achieved an importance in the hearts of the British nation which would in any case be impervious to new information! The overthrow of the French emperor in the aftermath of the battle signalled a long period of peace in Europe, for which Britain has always been eager to take the credit. Waterloo was also a forerunner of Britain's military involvement in Europe during the two World Wars of the twentieth century. The Battle of Waterloo was fought in Belgium, less than 30 miles from Mons, scene of the first major action between the British and German armies in the First World War. In both cases, the object of the British was the defence of Belgium. Hitler's conquest of Europe, which triggered the Second World War, was eerily reminiscent of Napoleon's military campaigns of 140 years earlier, up and including the invasion of Russia. In the Napoleonic Wars, as in the Second World War, the perception of the British was that they had to cross the Channel and deal with a dictator whom the rest of Europe had allowed to get out of hand.

There is another reason that the Battle of Waterloo has a special place in the nation's affections and that is because it is connected with the 'Invaders from the East' part of Britain's mythos. It ties in with Julius Caesar, William the Conqueror and the Spanish Armada – a threatened invasion from the Continent. Before the Battle of Trafalgar in 1805, Napoleon Bonaparte had been making active preparations for attacking Britain and ferrying an army across the Channel, with a view to marching on London. Mothers threatened their children that 'Boney' would get them, as though the emperor were some supernatural fiend. For a time, the fear lingered on that Napoleon represented a menace to the country. From this perspective, Wellington saved us from being overrun by foreign invaders and is consequently remembered with some of the gratitude which we accord Winston Churchill for rallying us against Hitler, another potential invader from the East. It is for this reason that both men have appeared on British £5 notes.

One final myth which was reinforced both during the run-up to the Battle of Waterloo and also during the fighting itself, was that of British sangfroid in the face of deadly peril. Two instances, one particularly well known, the other not quite as familiar, illustrate this. During the battle itself, the Earl of Uxbridge, the commander of Wellington's cavalry, was sitting on his horse near the Duke of Wellington. A French cannonball flew over the neck of Wellington's horse and went straight through Lord Uxbridge's leg, whereupon he said stoically, 'By God sir, I have lost my leg!' To which Wellington replied casually, 'By God sir, so you have!

We read earlier about the legend that Francis Drake had been playing bowls when the Armada was first sighted and had insisted on finishing the game before taking ship to deal with the Spanish and save Britain from invasion. A precisely similar tale is told of the Duke of Wellington when first he received news that Napoleon and his army were on the march towards him. On the night of 15 June 1815, just three days before the Battle of Waterloo, the wife of a senior British soldier held a ball in the Belgian capital, Brussels. It was later described as, 'the most famous ball in history', although of course the Duchess of Richmond could hardly have known that it would be anything special when she sent out the invitations.

Nobody knew what Napoleon planned to do and so when the Duke of Wellington arrived at the Duchess of Richmond's ball on 15 June, he could not have guessed that before supper, he would be handed a note informing him that the French army were on the move in the direction of Brussels and that they had already pushed aside a Prussian force which had tried to halt their advance. As overall leader of the Allied armies, one might have expected Wellington to react immediately to such shocking news. Instead, he read the note and then calmly went into supper, sitting next to Lady Georgiana, one of the Duchess of Richmond's daughters. Shortly after sitting down to eat, another note was brought to Wellington, which informed him that Napoleon's army had almost reached Quatre Bras, a strategic crossroads on the road to Brussels.

It is now that the parallel between Francis Drake and the Duke of Wellington emerges, because on receiving news which would have caused a lesser man to leap from his seat in alarm and begin rallying his army, Wellington continued to chat casually with the women on either side of him. It was not until twenty minutes after learning that the French were marching on Brussels that the Duke made his excuses to his hostess and announced that he was going to bed. In fact, he went privately to her husband and asked if he had a good map of the area around Brussels. The pair of them withdrew to the Duke of Richmond's dressing room, where together they examined the map. Wellington exclaimed, 'Napoleon has humbugged me, by God; he has gained twenty-four hours march on me'.

In short, the Battle of Waterloo taps into a number of the mythic themes which we have examined and it is for that reason that, along with 55 BC and 1066, 1815 became one of the most memorable years in British history, known to every schoolchild. Little wonder that it was important that it became a purely British victory, one so celebrated that one of London's biggest railway stations was later named in honour of it. Few people in Britain are aware, incidentally, that the Battle of Waterloo was not actually fought at Waterloo at all and that other countries have different names for the fighting which took place in Belgium that year. The fact is that Napoleon and his army never came within miles of Waterloo! The battle took place on farmland in and around a ridge called Mont St Jean. It is for this reason that in France the military action on 18 June 1815 is remembered by the name which Napoleon used for the encounter, *la Battaile de Mont-Saint-Jean*. This is itself a curious point and illustrates neatly, once again, why it is proper to refer to the 'myth' of Waterloo.

The Duke of Wellington had established his headquarters before the battle at the village of Waterloo, three miles from where the action would eventually take place. After the battle had been won, with the aid of the Prussian forces under the command of Marshal Blücher, the two commanders discussed what name should be given to the affair for posterity. By chance, their meeting took place outside an inn called *La Belle Alliance*. To Blücher, this seemed most fortuitous, as *Belle Alliance* suggested to him the alliance which had just defeated Napoleon; that of the Britain, Prussia, Austria, Russia and the other countries of the coalition ranged against France. When Blücher put this idea to Wellington, it was rejected out of hand. The Duke had already decided that the battle should be named after his own headquarters; even though they were miles from the scene of the actual fighting. Wellington had two reasons for this, the first being that he wished the battle to be named after *his* headquarters. His other purpose in insisting upon Waterloo was that he wanted his greatest victory to be a name that any Englishman would find easy to pronounce! The pronunciation of Waterloo is good deal more obvious than either Mont St Jean or Belle Alliance. Blücher agreed, but when he returned to Berlin, it was by the name of *Belle Alliance* that the victory became known to the Germans. That year, a square in Berlin was renamed *Belle-Alliance-Platz* to commemorate the battle, rather as we have in London Trafalgar Square, named after another famous victory of the Napoleonic Wars. By which it will be seen that even talking of the 'Battle of Waterloo' is, at least to some extent, subscribing to the myth created by the British.

The Battle of Waterloo was the climax of the Napoleonic Wars which had been plaguing the world since the end of the eighteenth century, when the thirty-year-old Napoleon had seized power in France with a *coup d'etat*. There are good grounds for seeing the Napoleonic Wars as the first 'world war', with the fighting ranging from the Caribbean to the Middle East, from southern Africa to Scandinavia. Going off at a slight tangent, it is curious to note that the three most notorious European dictators were none of them born in the countries of which they became the leaders. Stalin, ruler of Russia for thirty years, was from Georgia, Hitler was Austrian and Napoleon Bonaparte was born and grew up not in France, but Corsica.

When Napoleon became a dictator, first as consul and later as emperor, he ended the war with Britain which had been going more or less since the French Revolution took place. It did not, however, take long before his expansionist ambitions brought him once again into conflict with other European countries and also once more with Britain. For over ten years, the Napoleonic Wars raged across Europe and much of the world. Eventually, just as Hitler would do the following century, Napoleon over-reached himself and invaded Russia. It was a disastrous move. Gradually, his enemies hemmed him in until on 11 April 1814, Napoleon Bonaparte, Emperor of France, was forced to abdicate and went into exile on the little island of Elba, off the coast of Italy. A year later, he landed back in France and for the next three months, prepared for what was in effect a 'return bout' with the Allied armies. At the end of what became known as 'The Hundred Days', in which he once more consolidated his power in France, Napoleon had mustered his army and was marching west towards Belgium, hoping to reunite it with France, of which it was historically a part. Which of course was where the Duke of Wellington and the British army was stationed, waiting for him.

One point which deserves consideration when thinking about the outcome of Waterloo is the physical state of the emperor. All those years of campaigning and virtually living in the saddle had wrought a great and detrimental change upon the young man who had seized control of France in 1799. Some of those who saw Napoleon for the first time in a year at the Battle of Waterloo were shocked at the change in his appearance. Witnesses found him looking fatter and appearing much older than before his exile and it was also remarked that he seemed very lethargic and drowsy. At the most crucial action of his whole career, the commander of the French army did not appear to be altogether in control of himself. This was scarcely surprising when we examine his medical history.

Driven by his desire to occupy and rule the whole of Europe and beyond by force of arms, Napoleon's continuous military campaigns over the decades were scarcely conducive to good digestion. He snatched meals as and when possible and the food when travelling with his army was not always of high quality. The result was that from his mid-thirties, the emperor suffered from constant dyspepsia and colic. He also developed a peptic ulcer. The pain from these conditions was so excruciating that he was at times literally doubled up in agony. When at last the discomfort subsided, he found it necessary to sleep at once, no matter where he might be. At the Battle of Jena, which took place in Germany in 1806, his troops had to form a square around their slumbering commander, while the fighting raged.

Partly as a result of the colic, Napoleon's mind became more sluggish as the years passed. His impaired judgement nearly brought him to the brink of disaster on a number of occasions. Bladder problems too became a serious hindrance to Napoleon's military exploits. At Borodino, in 1812, he could barely ride because of the pain he was experiencing from his bladder. The technical name for the disorder from which Napoleon was suffering is dysuria, which makes urination difficult. It was well known among the troops who accompanied the emperor on campaign that from time to time they would have to halt, while their leader leaned against a tree for up to five minutes, struggling to empty his bladder. Then again, those years riding and sitting about in all conditions had given the emperor yet another debilitating disorder; that of prolapsed piles. We shall have occasion to return to this subject later, as Napoleon's health problems caused him to blunder badly at Waterloo. Wellington may have been a brilliant tactician, but at Waterloo all he really needed to do was stand fast and wait for his old enemy to make errors, which he duly did. The Duke of Wellington deserves credit for doing little other than holding his ground and waiting for his allies to arrive and save the day for him.

Having looked at the some of the background to the battle, we should acquaint ourselves with what forces were actually involved in the thing and what each side did, or failed to do. We will be examining in particular the claim made in almost every book on the subject published in Britain that the Duke of Wellington was in some sense the victor and responsible for beating

Napoleon that day, a victory upon which his political career and future reputation were founded. He went on to become Prime Minister twice.

Following the collapse of the French Empire, the restoration of the monarchy in France and the exile of the one-time emperor, there were quite a few loose ends to be tied up in Europe, matters relating to border disputes, national sovereignty and other questions to be settled as peace returned to the Continent. An international conference was set up to deal with these problems. The Congress of Vienna first met in November 1814 and passed its final act on 9 June 1815, a week before Napoleon's forces crossed the border and entered Belgium. This settlement laid the foundations for a century of peace in Europe. There were to be no more major European wars between this final act and the outbreak of the First World War in 1914. Various statesmen represented their countries at the Congress: Metternich for Austria, Tallyrand for France and, until Napoleon escaped from Elba, the Duke of Wellington on behalf of Britain. When it was known that Napoleon had returned to Paris and the newly-installed monarch of France had fled to Belgium, the countries represented at the Congress of Vienna hastily put together an army to tackle Napoleon, should he try once more to conquer Europe. The Russians, Austrians and Prussians maintained separate forces. It would take some time for Austria and Russia to mobilize their armies, but Wellington was given command of a mixed force of British, Dutch and German troops, totalling almost 70,000 men. In addition to this, the Prussians also had a separate army under the command of Blücher. This contributed another 50,000 troops to the forces facing Napoleon at Waterloo.

It is at this point that the myth of the 'British' victory at Waterloo begins to unravel in no uncertain fashion. The forces ranged against Napoleon on that fateful June day in 1815 consisted of just under 120,000 men. Of these, 31,000 belonged to the British Army, roughly a quarter. This is not the full story though. The 31,000 men who were nominally in the British army included 6,000 Germans in a unit known as the King's German Legion. It might be helpful at this point to explain what is meant by 'Germans' in this context. There was in 1815 no country called 'Germany'. Instead, there was a collection of city states and kingdoms, of which the most powerful and influential was Prussia. Another was Hanover, from where, of course, the British royal family had come in 1714. When Hanover was occupied by Napoleon's troops, the Hanoverian army had decamped to Britain, where they received a warm welcome from George III, he being the ruler of Hanover as well as the United Kingdom. These troops were formed into a special unit, the King's German Legion.

Adding up the Allied forces facing Napoleon in June 1815 reveals something which one would never guess from reading the average British schoolbook. There were 25,000 British, that is to say English, Welsh, Scots and Irish soldiers. Of the rest, 17,000 were Belgian and Dutch. It is when we add up those from what is modern-day Germany that the real surprise comes. In addition to the 6,000 Hanoverians of the King's German Legion, there were another 11,000 Hanoverian soldiers, 6,000 from Brunswick and another 3,000 from the minor state of Nassau. Then there were the 50,000 Prussians, whose role in the Battle of Waterloo was crucial. In total, there were that day ranged against Napoleon's army 79,000 troops from what we now call Germany and just 25,000 from Britain. In other words, more than three times as many Germans fought against the French at the Battle of Waterloo as did British soldiers! No wonder that this battle is remembered today in some parts of Europe as a German, rather than a British, victory.

Before the Battle of Waterloo, however, came two other battles which were to be of great importance in the final outcome of those June days in 1815. As soon as he left the Duchess of Richmond's ball, Wellington organized his forces and began making plans to protect Brussels by confronting Napoleon's army. The Prussian army under Blücher and the Anglo-Allied forces under Wellington both marched towards Napoleon and offered battle, positioning their forces to protect the route to Brussels. Not wishing to find himself fighting both armies simultaneously on the same field, Napoleon split his forces, attacking Wellington's and Blücher's armies separately. The way in which Napoleon directed his troops over those three days, culminating in his defeat at Waterloo, sheds yet more light on the idea of Wellington as the 'victor' at Waterloo and raises the possibility that his victory might have been at least as much due to his opponent's blunders, among other factors, as anything else.

Napoleon Bonaparte was a military and political genius who had risen to be dictator of France and then ruler of most of Europe. He had achieved this by a number of astonishing feats of arms against superior forces and also by very adroit manoeuvring on the diplomatic front. Even becoming the Emperor of France was a breathtaking accomplishment, when we consider that he was not French and did not learn to speak French until he began school in that country when he was ten. He spoke with a strong Corsican accent for the whole of his life. Seizing control of France at the age of thirty was incredible enough, but conquering large swathes of Europe over the next ten years and installing his brother on the throne of Spain was almost unbelievable. Little wonder that the epoch is named after such a man.

Napoleon may in his earlier years have been a military genius, but by 1815 his physical and intellectual powers were on the wane. Wellington observed in the aftermath of the Battle of Waterloo that there were none of the cunning and subtle tactics in the fighting which he might have expected from his arch-enemy and that Napoleon simply threw all his forces into frontal assaults against defended positions. It was obvious that little thought had been given to the tactics of this, the greatest battle of his career.

The first clash between Wellington and the French army took place at the crossroads of Quatre Bras on 16 June, the day following the Duchess of Richmond's famous ball. Napoleon wished at all costs to prevent Blücher from joining his forces with Wellington's Anglo-Allied army and so on the afternoon of the 16th, he took charge of the troops who would confront the Prussians, while leaving Marshal Ney, one of his most trusted men, to confront Wellington. It was assumed by all that these would be the battles which would decide the fate of France and perhaps even Europe. If things had gone badly, then there was nothing to stop Wellington and his British troops taking ship at Ostend and abandoning Brussels to Napoleon.

Marshal Blücher, commander of the Prussian army which Napoleon was determined to destroy on 16 June and the man whom some regard as the true victor of the Battle of Waterloo, was a strange and complex person. Held in enormous respect and affection by his men, Blücher had two nicknames, both indicative of how the soldiers he led thought of him. He was known commonly as '*Marschall Vorwarts*', 'Marshal Forwards.' This was due to Blücher's reputation for pressing forward at whatever cost. Not that he was one of those senior officers who 'lead from the rear'. One aspect of his character which caused the marshal to be so popular with his men was that Blücher was always likely to be in the thick of the fighting. The other name by which the head of the Prussian army was known was 'Papa Blücher', his men honestly seeing their leader as a substitute father. This feeling was warmly reciprocated by Blücher, who referred to the soldiers under his command as '*Meine kinder*', my children.

So far, so good and his troops could not hope for a more human officer to lead the Prussian army against Napoleon at this critical juncture in European affairs. There was a slight problem though and it was one which Wellington had encountered several times; namely that the 72-year-old Prussian marshal was prone to bouts of madness, the cause of which has never been properly explained. Seven years before Waterloo, for instance, Blücher became convinced that he had been raped by a French grenadier and that he was, as a consequence, pregnant with an elephant! He also told

Wellington on one occasion that his servants were in league with Napoleon and that they were making the floor of his quarters red hot. He coped by running across the floor quickly on tiptoe. Despite his mental problems, Blücher was a ferociously active man whose tenacity in attack on the battle-field was second to none.

Already, 48 hours before the contest at Waterloo, Napoleon showed that he was not the general he had once been. Having chosen to fight the Prussians himself, whom he found near the village of Ligny, while delegat-ing the attack on Wellington's forces to Marshal Ney, it was of course vital that efficient communications were established between the two parts of Napoleon's army. This was not done and as a result there were several fatal muddles, not only during the battles at Quatre Bras and Ligny on 16 June, but even at Waterloo itself. These suggested that Napoleon's failure to win at Waterloo had something to do with his own failing abilities, rather than Wellington's skills.

Marshal Ney, for all that he was popularly known as the 'Bravest of the Brave', behaved with a certain amount of timidity at Quatre Bras. Worse than that, in a foreshadowing of some of the French army's difficulties which would be seen at Waterloo, he did not obey the instructions which the emperor sent, at least not immediately. Ney had advanced towards the crossroad at Quatre Bras slowly and not with his usual élan. A small force of troops from Nassau blocked the way forward and Ney took a long time to deal with them. By the time that he arrived at the crossroads, Wellington and some of his army had already arrived and were prepared to hold the way against Ney. Because he had raced from Brussels as fast as he could, the Duke of Wellington had not been able to arrange for the whole of the Anglo-Allied army to accompany him to Quatre Bras. He had only 8,000 men to defend the position against the 28,000 troops commanded by Marshal Ney.

One does not need to be an expert on military tactics to see that with such a disparity of forces, Ney should have forged ahead and swept Wellington's soldiers aside. Had he done so, then the course of history might have been altered that day. He held back though, because he wanted to be quite sure that he had an overwhelming superiority. Specifically, he wished for the assistance of the 20,000 men of the I Corps, commanded by the Comte d'Erlon. Unfortunately for Marshal Ney, Napoleon wanted the I Corps as well, to throw against the right flank of the Prussians in the Battle of Ligny. Both men ordered d'Erlon to bring his troops to their aid at once and the poor man spent the afternoon of 16 June marching back and forth between Quatre Bras and Ligny, eventually taking part in neither battle! Had either

Napoleon or Ney had an extra 20,000 troops, then it is entirely possible that this would have tipped the balance and enabled either Wellington's or Blücher's army to be thoroughly routed. As it was, the results of both battles were inconclusive.

At Ligny, Napoleon simply mounted direct assaults at the centre of the Prussian army. This was very costly to the French, although it gradually wore down Blücher's troops. Blücher himself had his horse shot from under him. The animal crashed to the ground, trapping the marshal beneath it. Two cavalry charges then swept over the fallen horse and trapped rider, before 'Marshal Forwards' could be rescued. He may have been in his seventies, but Blücher still believed in leading from the front and not expecting his men to expose themselves to any danger which their commander was not prepared to brave himself.

Napoleon was renowned for his wide, flanking manoeuvres and simply hammering away in frontal assaults as he did at Ligny was uncharacteristic of his usual tactics. Had he had at his disposal the I Corps, no doubt he would have used it on the Prussian flanks, but their absence was really due to Napoleon's own failure to communicate clearly with the different parts of his army, something which would be seen again 48 hours later at Waterloo.

The Prussians were defeated at Ligny, but not crushed. They were able to retreat in good order, to fight again another day. At Quatre Bras, Wellington too was eventually forced to fall back to a defensible position on the ridge of Mont St Jean. His army too retreated carefully and was ready for the battle which would inevitably follow a few days later.

The day after the battles of Quatre Bras and Ligny were spent in preparation for what everybody knew would be the decisive encounter, one which would settle once and for all, one way or the other, Napoleon's claim to be the sole and legitimate ruler of France. There was heavy rain that night, 17 June. Just as at Agincourt and during the battle against the Spanish Armada, the weather would prove to be a crucial factor in British history.

When Napoleon rose and breakfasted at 6:00 am on 18 June, the rain had stopped, but it had left the ground sodden; which made the French emperor anxious that he would not be able to move his artillery easily. At this point, he faced only Wellington and his army. Marshal Grouchy had been despatched, along with 30,000 men, with the aim of herding Blücher's defeated army north, away from the coming confrontation between Napoleon and Wellington. All prudent military policy suggested that the French should now strike hard and fast at Wellington's forces, before there was any chance of their being reinforced. Instead, Napoleon, after having looked around the prospective battlefield, decided to go back to bed! His reason for doing so was that the ground would need to dry out a little before he would be ready to fight and that he had now done everything necessary to ensure victory. It will be remembered that this tendency to sleep at critical moments had been seen before.

It seems almost beyond belief that at 10:00 am on the day of the most important military engagement of his whole life, Napoleon should have chosen to go back to bed, but there it is. At the very moment that he should have been fighting to drive the Anglo-Allied army back towards Brussels, he was saying to his brother Jerome, 'I'm going to sleep till eleven. I'm sure to wake, but just in case I don't, you are to call me.' Most of us, even if we only had an appointment for a job interview of something of the sort for later in the day, would probably not return to our bed and ask our brother to call us later. That the Emperor of France should have done so at the very time that he should have been ordering a general advance is little short of incredible.

All this extra time was of great benefit to Wellington in arranging for the defence of the ridge of Mont St Jean. At the centre of his position was the farm of La Haie Sainte. The fighting did not actually begin until a little after midday and consisted in the main of the French conducting furious, frontal assaults on the Allied positions. So bloody was the fighting, that one of Wellington's officers observed afterwards that, 'I never heard yet of a battle in which every one was killed; but this seemed likely to be an exception.' Wellington's aim was simply to keep his forces where they were, blocking the road to Brussels. Even so, this modest aim was a fearful struggle in itself. By evening, the farmhouse of La Haie Sainte had fallen to the attackers and the Anglo-allied army was in terrible danger. Wellington was heard to mutter, 'Night or Blücher must come.' He knew that the most that he could hope to do was hang on grimly until something happened to relieve him.

The Prussian army led by Marshal Blücher had not been scattered at Ligny. Instead, it was now making its way inexorably towards the battle being fought for control of the ridge of Mont St Jean. This was the one thing which Napoleon had at all costs hoped to avoid, fighting Wellington's forces and Blücher's simultaneously. To this end, he had despatched Marshal Grouchy with thirty thousand men to chase the Prussians and stop them heading for the main battle. Unfortunately, the orders given to Grouchy were couched in vague terms and could equally well have allowed him to head for Mont St Jean as soon as he and his men could hear the cannon-fire from that direction. An extra 30,000 men in the early stages of the battle might have made a great difference to Napoleon's fortunes.

A large part of the trouble for Napoleon was that while the Duke of Wellington was riding around the field of battle, seeing for himself what was going on and delivering orders to officers at the scene of the heaviest fighting, Napoleon was for most of the time not even able to observe the battlefield directly. His piles were playing him up again. Although he did mount his horse at different times that day, it was not a comfortable experience for the emperor and he spent most of the time sitting in chairs. At his first headquarters that day, he had an armchair and when he moved forward to the Inn of Belle Alliance, an old wickerwork chair was procured, from which the seat had been partially removed to make it less awkward for the emperor's piles. A natural result of all this was that while Wellington could react instantly to any changing circumstance of battle, Napoleon was forced to send letters to his officers. By the time they received these written communications, the changing conditions of the battle had often made them irrelevant.

Wellington hung on like grim death, but the most that he might hope for was to fight the French army to a standstill. Victory, with the number of troops at his disposal, was simply not possible. It was not until later in the day when the Prussians under Blücher arrived, that any possibility of defeating Napoleon became likely. Once Blücher and his men did get to the fighting, the day turned into a rout for the French army. As the tens of thousands of Prussians swept towards them, even the Old Guard fled. It was the end of Napoleon's pretensions to be ruler of Europe, or indeed, even just France.

We have seen that Waterloo embodied several of the popular myths of the British; the 'Invaders from the East', Britain as the country which sorts out Europe's problems and so on. It also ties in with the story of the *Bounty*. What is the connection between a megalomaniac conqueror like Napoleon and the tragic figure of Fletcher Christian? The answer is that they were both, in their different ways, young rebels against the established order. Christian was twenty-three when he rose up against the authority of his superior officer and took over a ship of the Royal Navy. Napoleon was just thirty years of age when he launched a *coup d'état* and seized power in France. From this position, he challenged the old royal houses of Europe and dominated the Continent for a time. The man who defeated Napoleon was the very antithesis of rebellious idealism. The Duke of Wellington was almost a caricature of the diehard reactionary, especially in later years, when he tried to stifle the 1832 Reform Bill.

This conservative tradition, which the Duke of Wellington represented, triumphed at Waterloo and held sway for the next century. The peace which Europe enjoyed in the nineteenth century was that established by the Congress of Vienna and helped to ensure that revolution never really got off the ground in Europe until the well into the twentieth century. British caution and innate conservatism therefore shaped the course of European, and also world, history until 1914. It was founded upon the clash of the youthful and idealistic Corsican and the steady and reactionary British aristocrat.

Chapter 6

Florence Nightingale in Scutari 1854–1855: 'A Lady with a Lamp shall stand, In the great history of the Land'

lorence Nightingale is the very epitome of one of the British mythic archetypes at which we have been looking. She is the personification of the little person who takes on authority, standing up to the leadership of the British Army at the height of the Empire and bending them to her will. At a time when a woman's place was most definitely in the home, here was one woman who not only refused to stay at home, but actually went to war in order to protect the welfare of wounded and ill men. The 'Lady of the Lamp' is the closest thing which the British have to a national heroine. She has even been awarded the accolade of appearing on the currency; from 1975 to 1994, Florence Nightingale was to be found on £10 notes, leading to that denomination becoming colloquially known as a 'Nightingale'.

There can surely be very little to say on the subject of Florence Nightingale's work; this, after all, is the woman responsible for the establishment of nursing in its modern form. She raised nursing from being the occupation of drunken slatterns such as Sarah Gamp, in Dickens' *Martin Chuzzlewit*, to the honourable profession which it is today.

The difficulty with criticizing and deconstructing the myth of Florence Nightingale and her activities in Turkey is that it makes many people feel uncomfortable. It seems almost churlish and small-minded, a century and a half after her work, to pick apart and quibble over the details of what she actually achieved. After all, it must surely be indisputable that she at least did more good than bad and that the lot of those casualties of the Crimean War would have been far less pleasant and considerably more hazardous, had Florence Nightingale not taken charge of the hospital at Scutari? This is certainly the view of most people today. Here is what a popular children's history book, published by the Oxford University Press, has to say on the matter:

> Florence Nightingale became a national heroine when she took a group of nurses with her to the Crimea. At the army hospital at

Scutari she and her nurses reduced the death rate from 42 per cent to 2 per cent, through attention to cleanliness, diet and adequate supplies.

Or consider this, from the *Cambridge Biographical Encyclopaedia*:

After the Battle of Alma (1854), led a party of 38 nurses to organize a nursing department at Scutari. There she found grossly inadequate sanitation, but she soon established better conditions and had 10,000 wounded under her care.

The take-home message from all this appears to be that whatever Florence Nightingale did, she saved lives, which can of course only be a good thing. No mention by the way, in that entry from the *Cambridge Biographical Encyclopaedia*, that of those '10,000 wounded under her care', no fewer than half subsequently died in her hospital, the vast majority from diseases which they contracted there rather than from the wounds which they had suffered on the battlefield. The mortality rate at that wonderfully clean hospital in Scutari, of which we have all heard, was a staggering 50 per cent.

We shall look later at just what it was that this celebrated woman was doing during the Crimean War, about which, many people today seem very vague. Everybody knows that she fought hard to get supplies for the men in the care of her nurses and that the Army opposed her and made life difficult for her, but apart from that, what did she actually *do*? Was she emptying bedpans and bandaging up wounded soldiers? Many of us know that she was held in high regard by ordinary rank-and-file soldiers, but for doing what? Acting on their behalf against uncaring officers? Saving their lives? The details are, for most of us, more than a little hazy.

What Florence Nightingale did and did not achieve will be considered later in this chapter, but before this we should pause and consider the unpalatable fact that the death-rate in that famous hospital in Scutari, a suburb of modern-day Istanbul, was actually higher than that at any other of the hospitals run by the British Army during the Crimean War and that this was due largely to the efforts of Florence Nightingale. In other words, her arrival at Scutari triggered a surge in deaths at the hospital, which went on for six months and was only halted when the Army stepped in and took their own measures to combat disease. This is, to say the very least of it, not something which is generally known!

This view incidentally, that the effect of Florence Nightingale's work was to increase the number of deaths at Scutari, is not that of some modern-day, revisionist historian. It was Nightingale's own opinion and the realization that she had done more harm than good during the Crimean War was to be the driving force in her later life. Writing two years after the end of the war to Sir John MacNeill, the man in charge of the Supplies Commission, Florence Nightingale freely admitted that the death rate from dysentery on the wards in her own hospital had been at least 25 per cent higher than those in front-line military hospitals in the Crimea and that the reason was that disease had been 'generated within the building itself'.

What is sad is that the popular view of Florence Nightingale as the 'Lady With The Lamp' of the Crimean War blinds us to her very real achievements in the field of feminism and also that of research and statistics. She really was a remarkable person, but for reasons of which hardly anybody today has even heard. To see why this should be, we will have to look at the Crimean War and try to understand the effect which it had on Victorian Britain. It is not an edifying story and the fact that the only two incidents which we remember 150 years later are both miserable failures tells us a great deal. You would be hard-pressed to find anybody in this country now who could tell you a single thing about the Crimean War, other than the name of Florence Nightingale and the fact that the Charge of the Light Brigade took place in the course of the conflict.

The real cause of the Crimean War is simple to understand and twenty-first century readers should have no difficulty in seeing just why a British army was despatched to the Crimean peninsula to face the Russians. There had for some time, in the mid-nineteenth century, been a fear by the British government that the Russian Empire was trying to exercise too much control in the Eastern Mediterranean and this might have had an adverse effect on British interests. There was also a supposed threat to India, which was a British possession at that time. All this has a very modern flavour to it, the fear of subversion in Afghanistan and the need for Russia to maintain warm-water ports in the Black Sea. As recently as 2014, Russian desire to maintain control of the port of Sevastopol led to the invasion and annexation of the Crimea.

The *Casus Belli* in 1853 came with a dispute over the guardianship of the Christian holy places in Jerusalem, specifically whether the French or Russians should exercise this control. After Russia destroyed some Turkish ships, Britain and France declared war on Russia on 28 March 1854. In the late summer, British and French forces landed in the Russian territory of the Crimea and the war began in earnest.

The Crimean War has been called the first 'modern' war, in that tele-
graphs, photography and steamships were used in it. There were two other
innovations which had even greater influence on future military operations.
Firstly, trench warfare, which was to play such an important role in the First
World War, was a feature also of the Crimean. The other was the presence
of war correspondents, whose despatches could be sent back to their own
countries within seconds and printed in the next day's newspapers. This
rapid exchange of information could work the other way too, with facts
being transmitted to any enemy almost instantaneously.

In 1854, the War Ministry in London issued details of the forces being
sent to the Black Sea, including the precise numbers of troops. In a patriotic
fervour, *The Times* newspaper printed all this, to show how well-equipped
and numerous was the army going off to war with Russia. During the
Napoleonic War, the troops would have arrived at the front long before
this information would be available to any enemy. With modern technology
though, the Russians were able to buy a copy of *The Times* and then relay
the facts and figures to the government in St Petersburg at the speed of
light, via the telegraph lines which now covered Europe. As the British
Commander-in-Chief observed bitterly, 'the enemy never spends a farthing
for information. He gets it all for five pence from a London paper.'

It was *The Times* and their reporter in the Crimea who were largely
responsible for creating the Florence Nightingale myth as it has come down
to us today. William Howard Russell kept readers in Britain fully appraised
of the woefully inadequate nature of the provision made for the soldiers
being sent to the Crimea, from deficiencies in their diet to the lack of warm
clothing and medical care. Some of the shortages were truly scandalous.
things such as blankets and coats. This caused great indignation in Britain
and collections were organized for the soldiers of both money and warm
clothing.

Even boots were in short supply. Most of those supplied by the various
firms contracted by the army were not able to cope with very muddy or wet
conditions and the Crimean peninsula in winter was both very wet and hor-
ribly muddy. The boots worn by the soldiers simply fell to pieces and when it
was found that the Russians were furnishing their troops with better quality
footwear, the British troops resorted to looting bodies or even grave robbing.
One sailor, Midshipman Evelyn Wood, paid a member of his ship's crew ten
shillings to visit a graveyard and find him a pair of Russian boots.

Lack of clothing and footwear was bad enough, but it was the treatment, or lack of it, for those wounded in battle which really inflamed public

opinion. Newspaper readers in London, including cabinet ministers, were able to learn from *The Times* that 'There were not sufficient surgeons; no dressers and no nurses; no linen for bandages – and yet, no one was to blame.'

There was outrage and demands grew for something to be done about the scandalous situation. In particular, people were looking to the Secretary at War, Sidney Herbert, for decisive action. Victorian Britain was famous for the way in which jobs were distributed more on the basis of social position than ability and it was at this point that the Secretary at War recalled that he had a very useful friend from a respectable family who might be able to help out with the medical problems facing the army in the Crimea.

Florence Nightingale is renowned for being a gadfly in the side of the Establishment. We have most of us heard of her struggles with senior officers who regarded her and her nurses with contempt and how she struggled against complacency and sloth, always sticking up for the welfare of the ordinary soldier against his uncaring superior officers. She is the very archetype of the little person who fights against authority with tenacity and ultimately wins through sheer persistence. This is a very misleading image, because Florence Nightingale was in fact a personal friend of the Secretary at War and it was he who commissioned her to travel to Turkey and take charge of the hospital there.

Sidney Herbert was the son of the Earl of Pembroke and for much of his life he ran the family estate at Wilton in Wiltshire. One of his neighbours in Wiltshire was a very wealthy man called William Nightingale. Nightingale had two daughters and when Sidney Herbert was on his honeymoon in Rome, he got to know one of these young women very well, 28-year-old Florence. It was to be the beginning of a long friendship, which would perhaps prove more beneficial to Florence Nightingale than it would to Sidney Herbert. When he died at the relatively young age of fifty-one, there were some who said that he had been driven to an early grave by the incessant demands of his friend and collaborator, Florence Nightingale.

Both Florence and her sister had been born while her parents were travelling around Italy and they were named after the cities in which they had been born. Before Florence Nightingale became famous, Florence had traditionally been a man's name and it was her example which made it an acceptable name for girls. Her father educated her at home and from the beginning, she made it clear that she had no intention of following the normal way of life of a girl born into a very well-to-do family, that is to say marrying a wealthy and respectable man and then settling down to run a house and raise a family. Florence felt that she was called by God to do something more with her life than just settling down to a life of cosy domesticity. She travelled across Europe with friends of her father, visiting various hospitals, before going on to Egypt. In Egypt, she clearly heard God speak to her, calling Florence Nightingale into His service, and on her return to England, her parents were at last persuaded to allow her to spend a few months studying nursing in Germany. Those four months in 1851 at an establishment for Protestant deaconesses in Kaiserwerth were the only training in medicine which she received.

Because the majority of nurses in Britain were of very poor quality, with a reputation for immorality and slovenliness, it was perhaps not surprising that a woman from a good family, with independent means of her own, should have appeared eminently suited to manage a philanthropic nursing home in London called the Establishment for Gentlewomen During Illness. This was a nursing home for upper-class women who had fallen on hard times and in August 1853, Florence Nightingale was appointed to manage it, which she did very successfully.

To sum up then, Florence Nightingale was an enthusiastic amateur with a great interest in medicine, but little practical knowledge or experience. Her talent lay in organizing and getting things done, rather than emptying bedpans and taking pulses. She had an income of her own of £500 a year, equivalent perhaps to £40,000 today. This meant that at a pinch she was able to pay for necessary materials from her own pocket and she also had the resources of her very wealthy family behind her, in addition to the backing of various important people, including cabinet ministers who happened to be personal friends. It is not to be wondered at that when Secretary at War Sidney Herbert found himself being increasingly criticized for the deficiencies of medical care for the army in the Crimea, this well-connected and well-off woman should have seemed the ideal person to take a group of nurses out to the war and care for some of the wounded soldiers.

One final point needs to be considered about Florence Nightingale and that is that she had not the faintest idea what caused people to become ill or suffer infections. This was not her fault: most doctors were hazy about this themselves at the time, but it was to have a bearing on how able she was to run a hospital safely and save the lives of the patients there. There were two chief theories of the causation of disease at that time. One of these was the correct one, that illnesses and infections are caused by microscopic germs, bacteria and viruses. The other was the miasma theory. This held that it was 'bad air' which made people ill and that if you could only ensure access to plenty of fresh air, free from bad smells, then diseases such as smallpox and cholera would not afflict them. Florence Nightingale was fanatically keen on the virtues of fresh air and good diet and felt that it was the lack of these which made people fall ill. It was a disastrous error into which to fall and this quite false belief was to cost the lives of thousands of the men whom she was sent to look after.

Conditions at the two large hospitals at Scutari, near modern-day Istanbul, were unbelievably grim. When Florence Nightingale and her thirty-eight nurses arrived there on 4 November 1854, a little over a week after the Battle of Balaclava had been fought, there were practically no blankets, bedclothes or nightwear for the men brought to the Barracks Hospital at Scutari. Many of them used their muddy boots as pillows at night and covered themselves in the filthy and bloodstained greatcoats which they had worn during the fighting. Some slept on the floor.

Many of the men brought from the Crimea to the Barracks Hospital at Scutari had wounds which became badly infected and, there being no antibiotics at the time, this resulted in either blood poisoning or gangrene. Blood poisoning killed, but gangrene could be treated. The remedy for gangrene then, as now, was the amputation of the affected parts. If this is not done, then the rotting of the flesh will spread until the patient dies. Amputations at Scutari were carried out without either anaesthetics or antiseptic procedures. One of the patients at Scutari at the time of Florence Nightingale's arrival was an officer called Alexander Moore, whose bed was by a window and afforded him a perfect view of the courtyard which lay near to the room where the amputations were being carried out. He described how as he watched, bloody arms and legs were casually disposed of by the simple expedient of being thrown out of the window, where they built up into a ghastly heap. Pigs kept by local people were allowed to scavenge freely in the environs of the Barracks Hospital and rooted among the amputated limbs, actually feeding on human flesh within sight of the patients. (The scene at Balaclava was even worse. It was said that so many amputations were performed in the aftermath of the battle in October, that the harbour was clogged with human arms and legs.)

Florence Nightingale's own words describe what she found at the hospital that November:

> Underneath its imposing mass were sewers of the worst possible construction, from which the wind blew sewer air up into the corridors where the sick were lying. Wounds and sickness, overcrowding and want of proper ventilation added to the foulness of the

atmosphere. At night it was indescribable. The wards were infested with rats, mice and vermin. Even the commonest utensils for cleanliness, decency and comfort were lacking . . . not a basin, not a towel, not a bit of soap or a broom. The cooking was done in three large coppers at one end of the building, and it took three or four hours to serve the ordinary dinners.

This appraisal illustrates two of Florence Nightingale's main concerns, the things which she felt caused illness. One was a lack of fresh, wholesome air and the other inadequate nutrition. When she writes of 'sewer air', she refers essentially to bad smells. That meals took three hours to arrive in the wards from the kitchen might be regrettable, but will not make anybody catch a disease. Infectious illnesses are spread by contaminated water or contact with an infected person. It was ignorance of this fact which prevented any real improvement in the conditions of the hospitals which Florence Nightingale supervised.

It is now time to consider what Florence Nightingale did and did not achieve at Scutari. She and her nurses were shocked beyond measure by the terrible state of the hospitals and at once set to work cleaning them and improving the quality of life for the men. To this end, they scrubbed floors, provided bed-linen, cleaned the latrines and devoted their efforts towards making the lives of the patients more comfortable in every way. Nothing was allowed to stand in the way of this endeavour and this is where Florence Nightingale's public image began to be forged, as the opponent of pettifogging rules and regulations. For instance, while most of the soldiers in the hospital were sleeping in their dirty uniforms, a consignment of 27,000 shirts had been landed, but could not be opened without the authorization of the Board of Survey. There was no telling when this might be obtained, so Florence Nightingale ordered the bundles of shirts to be opened and the clothing delivered to the hospital, 'red tape or no red tape', as she put it. Such high-handed actions did little to endear her to senior officers, but earned the gratitude of the ordinary soldiers.

From her own money, Florence Nightingale started a laundry, and kitchens were set up to provide the men at Scutari with nourishing hot meals: in a hundred different ways, their existence was changed out of all recognition. Not only were their physical needs catered for, but thought was also given to supplying books and games while they convalesced after treatment. Instead of the curt letters which the families of soldiers usually received to notify them of the death of a loved one, 'Dear Mrs Smith, we regret to inform you that your son John has died in action . . .', Florence Nightingale spend many hours composing and writing long and detailed letters to wives and mothers; telling them of the last hours of their relatives.

There can be not the least doubt that this remarkable woman was beloved by the men for whom she cared. The whole atmosphere of the Barracks Hospital was transformed. One soldier wrote a letter home in which he said that, 'Before she came, there was cussin' and swearin', but after that it was as holy as a church'. She went through the wards at night, checking that everything was well and stopping to talk to men and comfort the dying. It was in this way that the image of the Lady with the Lamp arose, for she carried with her on her nightly rounds a little Chinese lantern.

A report in *The Times* popularized the image of the 'Lady with the Lamp' as did a poem written two years later by Longfellow. In *The Times*, it was said that: 'When all the medical officers have retired for the night and silence and darkness have settled down upon those miles of Prostrate sick, she may be observed alone, with a little lamp in her hand, making her solitary rounds.' It was said that the soldiers kissed her shadow as she passed. In 1857, the year after the Crimean War ended, the American poet Henry Wadsworth Longfellow, famous for his epic narrative poem *The Song of Hiawatha*, wrote a shorter piece which was dedicated to Florence Nightingale. This poem was called *Santa Filomena* and it helped to spread the image of Florence Nightingale as the 'Lady with the Lamp'. One verse of Longfellow's poem reads:

> A Lady with a Lamp shall stand,
> In the great history of the land,
> A noble type of good, Heroic womanhood.

Florence Nightingale's life was one of selfless devotion to what she perceived as the needs of others and it is not at all too strong for the case to describe her as a heroine. And yet we come now to some uncomfortable facts. For all the scrubbing and cleaning which she and her nurses undertook, despite the provision of clean bed-linen and hot food, in defiance of the increased pleasantness of their surroundings, the patients in the Barracks Hospital at Scutari continued to die at an alarming rate. Indeed, the only noticeable effect of Florence Nightingale's presence at the hospital was that the death rate actually increased the longer that she was in charge of the hospital, until by February 1855, when the nurses had been working hard to improve conditions for four months, the death had risen to 42 per cent. Almost half the men brought to the hospital were dying from infections which they acquired in the hospital itself. It is doubtful if Florence Nightingale's work saved a single patient's life.

In effect, the establishment which Florence Nightingale was super-intending was not a hospital at all, but rather a hospice, where ill people came to die in the most agreeable surroundings which could be contrived. Whatever she did, the mortality rate at Scutari rose inexorably and it was obvious to everybody except her and her nurses that she was not contribut-ing in the slightest degree to the recovery or cure of any of the men sent to the hospital which she was running.

There was no incentive at all for this information to become widely known and even today, there is a general impression that Florence Nightingale was doing grand work during the Crimean War, tending and healing all those poor soldiers. In fact, she presided over what a modern writer has described as a 'death camp'. For the Victorians reading their newspapers though, the Lady with the Lamp was just what they wanted to hear about. After all the stories about inadequate supplies for the troops, to say nothing of military disasters such as the Charge of the Light Brigade, this was 'feel-good' stuff, a plucky little woman who was fighting officialdom and acting the part of a ministering angel. The people back in Britain couldn't hear enough about her and she swiftly became a celebrity.

By February, with the death rate at Scutari still rising, it was obvious that something would have to be done about Florence Nightingale's hos-pital. The government sent out the most unromantically-named Sanitary Commission to see what needed to be done and then to do it. In January 1855, the government led by Lord Aberdeen had resigned over the conduct of the Crimean War, which meant that Secretary at War Sidney Herbert was replaced. Of course, Florence Nightingale was a protégé of Herbert's and with his departure a new man, Lord Panmure, was appointed. It was decided almost at once that something really needed to be done about all those thousands of soldiers dying at the Barracks Hospital.

In March 1855 the Sanitary Commission, consisting of two doctors and an engineer, arrived at Scutari. Their instructions were clear and explicit. They were not there merely to make enquiries, but rather to examine the situation and then immediately take whatever action they deemed necessary. Nor were they to rely upon others to carry out their instructions, but were to supervise the work themselves. Matters at the hospital where Florence Nightingale had been given a free hand for months had reached such a crisis point, that something had to be done at once. The written orders to the three men who composed the commission including the unambiguous statement that: 'It is important that you are deeply impressed with the necessity of not resting content with an order, but that you see instantly, by yourselves or your agents, to the commencement of the work, and to its superintendence day by day until it is finished.' It is difficult to escape the feeling that the new Secretary at War felt that by trusting the management of a military hospital to a keen amateur who happened to be a personal friend, his predecessor had been more than a little irresponsible.

Let there be no doubt about what had happened. Various history books, even those published in recent years, still repeat the myth, as propagated in the 1850s, that when she arrived at Scutari, Florence Nightingale found that the death rate at the hospital was 42 per cent and that by her Herculean efforts, this had been reduced to a trifling 2 per cent. What had actually happened was that in the months that she had been working at the Barracks Hospital at Scutari, the death rate had *risen* to 42 per cent and that this crisis had precipitated the despatch of a commission from London charged with finding out what was wrong at Scutari and then putting it right as a matter of urgency.

It is not difficult in retrospect to see why the nurses at Scutari were unable to prevent epidemics of infectious bowel diseases from killing almost half the men sent to the hospitals there. Although Florence Nightingale was on the right track in scrubbing and cleaning the wards and arranging for clothes to be washed regularly, she was really only tinkering with the symptoms of the problem, rather than tackling the cause. We know that wherever she had a hand in matters, this dedicated woman was fanatical about allowing as much fresh air into sickrooms as could possibly be managed. It was her avowed aim that the air inside hospitals should be as fresh and sweet-smelling as that outside. The reason for this obsession was that Florence Nightingale thought that bad smells from decaying organic matter had the power to make people ill. This was what she meant when she referred to 'sewer air', that the smell of faeces could, by itself, actually spread dysentery.

There was nothing strange about this adherence to the miasma theory of disease: it was held by many eminent doctors, although some were already beginning to champion the alternative idea of contagion by germs. In Germany, Ignaz Semmelweis had already worked out that contagion could take place through contact and was advocating the antiseptic precaution of hand-washing to stop disease being transmitted in this way. This was seven years before Florence Nightingale sailed off to take charge at Scutari. In London, Dr John Snow had published in 1849 an essay called *On the Mode of Communication of Cholera*. Dr Snow was later to demonstrate that cholera was carried in water, rather than wafting up into the air, borne on the smell of bad drains. The miasma theory was thought to part of a general principle of nature, with medical professors in the early nineteenth century even applying it to nutrition. The fact that many butchers were fat was believed to be caused by their smelling meat all day long, rather than the fact that they were probably a little too fond of pork chops and sausages!

Of course, a keen and well-meaning amateur like Florence Nightingale could hardly be expected to be up-to-date with modern theories and recent developments in the field of medicine. She was not, after all, a doctor. Most people still saw an association between bad smells and illness and in embracing this idea, she was only subscribing to the generally-held belief. For Florence Nightingale though, there was a little bit more to the miasma than just as a physical cause of illness. She believed that God had created miasmas so that humanity might learn about them through studying the natural world, so at the same time discovering how to cope with and prevent disease. For her, nursing was a form of natural theology, and those working like her with ill people had an unparalleled opportunity for spiritual growth, as they found out about God by learning the 'laws of health'. This religious devotion to a false theory relating to the transmission of disease was unfortunate, because having once received this information as a form of divine revelation, one could hardly expect a devout woman like Florence Nightingale to abandon it on the strength of later and more convincing evidence.

This mistaken understanding of the means by which illness really spreads, led Florence Nightingale to take steps which exacerbated the situation at Scutari and bring about even more deaths. Having tidied up the Barracks Hospital to a great extent, she thought that it would be better for soldiers wounded in the fighting to be shipped across the Black Sea, so that they could be allowed to stay in her hospital, rather than in those nearer to the battlefield. In addition to the 'miasma' causing illness, Florence Nightingale attributed the ill health of men in hospital to poor diet. Since she was now providing nourishing hot meals for them, it seemed obvious to her that patients would be better off in her own establishment, rather than one near the battlefield which might not have adequate arrangements for catering.

There were two problems here, the first of which being that there was a high mortality rate on the sea voyage from the Crimea to Turkey. Secondly, the more crowded the hospital became and the more closely packed were the patients, the more likely they were to catch diseases from each other. The wards might have been swept regularly, been better ventilated, cleaner and in general look more aesthetically pleasing, the men might have been

1. Queen Victoria and Prince Albert as medieval monarchs.

2. A bad-tempered King John reluctantly signs the Magna Carta.

3. The White Man's Burden; bringing British values to the world.

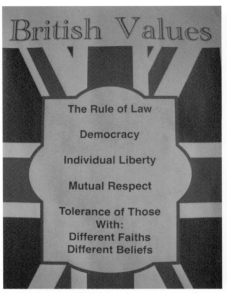

4. Fundamental British values, supposedly derived from the Magna Carta.

5. The real Henry V: not a bit like Laurence Olivier or Kenneth Branagh.

6. The mud of both the Western Front and also Agincourt.

7. Henry V's chivalry in action: prisoners of war having their throats cut.

8. Francis Drake playing bowls; a towering figure in British mythology.

9. Commemorative plaque on the house in South London once occupied by 'Captain' Bligh.

10. 'Captain' Bligh and some of his crew are cast adrift in a small boat, following the mutiny on the *Bounty*.

11. Marshal Blücher, the true victor at Waterloo.

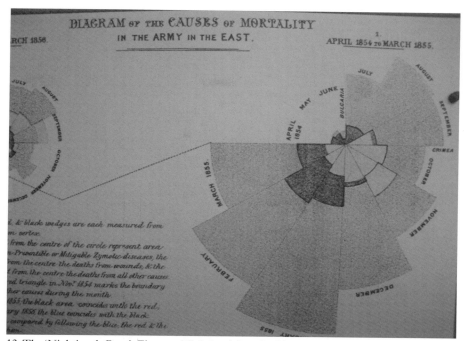

12. The 'Nightingale Rose'. Florence Nightingale's real achievement was in statistics, rather than nursing.

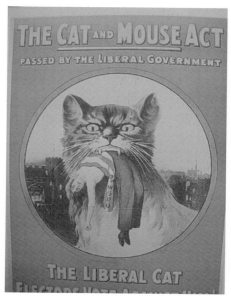

13. The suffragettes as helpless victims, rather than dangerous terrorists.

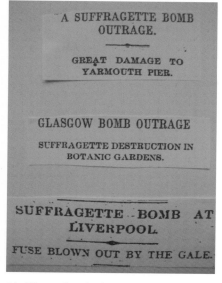

14. The authentic face of the suffragettes: newspaper reports of bomb attacks in 1913.

15. The popular image of Edwardian Britain: wealthy ladies at Ascot in 1905.

16. The reality of Edwardian Britain: lines of soldiers advance on strikers, as police follow in an armoured car.

17. Over the top: British troops march across No Man's Land towards the waiting German machine guns.

18. General Haig; callous butcher or brilliant strategist?

19. A Spitfire from the Battle of Britain, piloted by a Polish airman.

20. One of the Chain Home radar towers which were of crucial importance during the Battle of Britain.

provided with board games and books, but without a clear understanding of how germs can be spread via contaminated water and bodily contact, it was inevitable that more and more of them should fall sick.

When the Sanitary Commission, headed by Dr John Sutherland and accompanied by a civil engineer called Robert Rawlinson, began work at Scutari in March 1855, it was plain to them what needed to be done to reduce the catastrophic death rate. This had no reference either to diet or any so-called 'miasma'. The sewers beneath the Barracks Hospital were in an appalling state, blocked up and forming a reservoir of disease which was the real reason for the endemic dysentery which afflicted the patients there. Fortunately, the Commission had orders not only to inspect, but also to act on what they found. The sewers were flushed out and it was now that the death rate dropped from 42 per cent to 2 per cent – it had absolutely nothing whatsoever to do with Florence Nightingale and her nurses.

The myth of Florence Nightingale had by that time already began its unstoppable growth. There were a number of reasons for this. In the first place, the news from the Crimea had been unremittingly grim and the idea that here was a ready-made heroine was an appealing one to the publishers of newspapers and magazines. It is likely that the physical resemblance which Florence Nightingale bore to Queen Victoria worked too to the advantage of the myth-makers. Both were slightly-built women, whose faces showed a steely determination. Inevitably, comparisons were drawn between them.

The newspapers, especially *The Times,* had been telling people almost from the opening shots of the war that the Army was mismanaging matters and that something needed to be done for the soldiers. Here was a little woman apparently able to work miracles and quite unafraid to take on the senior officers and sort out those things which they themselves were either unable or unwilling to do. This chimed well with the idea of the small person standing up to authority, a mythic archetype for which the British have always had a soft spot.

There was also something fascinating about the novel idea of a woman acting vigorously outside the domestic sphere, which was not at all common in Victorian Britain. There had been the occasional woman like Elizabeth Fry who undertook philanthropic work in the public sphere, but Florence Nightingale's exploits were in a different league. The time was ripe for some good and heartening news from a badly-fought war and this woman was it!

The myth of Florence Nightingale as the 'Lady with the Lamp' is disquieting for several reasons. There is, to begin with, something more than a little distasteful about celebrating the supposed achievements of a woman who set out to improve a hospital and then did little other than make dying patients comfortable, without actually extending their lives. This was done in the name of God, who both called Florence Nightingale to take up nursing and then showed her a thoroughly wrongheaded idea about how disease spread.

There is also the way in which the myth, as it still circulates, has the effect of perpetuating gender stereotypes, whereas one of Florence Nightingale's real accomplishments was to help break down those very stereotypes about the proper place of women in society. The pernicious influence of the image of a woman who epitomized a certain view of femininity, as encapsulated by Longfellow when he wrote, 'A noble type of good, Heroic womanhood', lingers on. We remember Florence Nightingale not for her very real achievements, all of which were made years after the Crimean War, but rather for men kissing her shadow and blessing her name as though she were an angel.

In Victorian Britain, an ideological belief was widely held by all classes that there were, and should be, 'separate spheres' for the activities of men and women. For men, the proper sphere was public life: work, university, law, economics, politics, science and art. Women, on the other hand, were thought best suited to the private sphere of the home. Domesticity and child-rearing were believed to be their natural destiny. It was against this strongly-prevailing view that Florence Nightingale fought. The idea of women eschewing married life to pursue a career was thought of as perverse and an attempt to overthrow the natural order of things. Nurses before Florence Nightingale were frequently viewed as morally suspect for precisely this reason, that they inhabited the public rather than the private sphere. Rumours of nurses having sex with male patients and drinking heavily were common. It was not to be wondered at: nice women stayed at home and looked after the house and children. Once they spent their days out and about with strange men, there was no telling where it would end!

Before Florence Nightingale's example, it was fine for middle-class girls to become governesses; this was still essentially operating in the domestic sphere, rather than in the world at large. Domestic service for working-class girls was also respectable for the same reason. But now it had been shown that a woman could do something useful in the public eye, even have her exploits reported by *The Times*. Even that most conservative of people, Queen Victoria, approved of her actions, which mattered enormously at that time. Victoria wrote to Florence Nightingale in Scutari, saying, 'It will be a great satisfaction to me, when you return at last to these shores, to make the acquaintance of one who has set so bright an example to our sex.' The statesman Lord Stanley, wrote, 'Mark what, by breaking through customs and prejudices, Miss Nightingale has effected for her sex. She has opened to them a new profession, a new sphere of usefulness.'

This then is one lasting contribution made by Florence Nightingale which has today been all but forgotten. Most people have heard of Emmeline Pankhurst in connection with the struggle for female emancipation: few realize the role which Florence Nightingale played in that same cause. Fifty years before the suffragettes were active, here was a woman who demonstrated to Victorian society that women could be as useful in the public sphere as they were in the domestic. Nor was that all that Florence Nightingale showed. Her influence in another field has also faded from memory, obscured by that dreadful, mawkish image of the 'Lady with the Lamp'.

Florence Nightingale was educated at home by her father and never attended school. She was an apt pupil and studied classics and mathematics in her teens to a very high standard. After her return from the Crimean War, she set out to discover just what had gone wrong at the hospitals which she had been supervising. It is a tribute to her honesty that whatever others might have claimed on her behalf, she herself never said that she had reduced the death rates at Scutari. On her return from the war, Florence Nightingale decided to analyse the meticulous records which she had kept at the hospitals at which she had worked and see what they might say about the comparative mortality rates and spread of disease. To do this, it would first be necessary to learn statistics.

William Farr was an epidemiologist, regarded today as one of the earliest experts on medical statistics. It was to this man Florence Nightingale turned when she wished to be taught about studying the data which she had collected during the Crimean War. It did not take her long to see that the existing ways of displaying such information in the form of charts and tables would not really be sufficient for her needs. She wanted visual representations which would make the dry figures come to life in a way that a list of numbers, one above the other, never could. Every schoolchild in the country benefits from the methods which Florence Nightingale used in her reports. She seized upon a then little-known method of displaying numerical information. This was to compare quantities by showing them as proportional segments of a circle; the technique which is known today as 'pie charts'. She did not, contrary to one popular legend, invent the pie chart, but was certainly responsible for popularizing it.

The type of pie chart which Florence Nightingale really made her own was the 'Nightingale Rose' or coxcomb chart, technically known as 'polar area diagrams'. In these, an example of which may be seen in Illustration 12, the sections are of equal angles and it is the varying radii which indicate the magnitude of the figures. This type of diagram is used to show cyclic changes, in this case, the monthly death rate from various diseases. For her work in this field, Florence Nightingale was in 1858 elected a member of the Statistical Society of London, which later became the Royal Statistical Society. She was the first female member of this organization, which showed once more that women's work need not necessarily be only in the domestic sphere.

One of the things which her statistical analysis of the Crimean War death rates showed was that in the wards controlled by Florence Nightingale, the number of men dying was far higher than the front-line hospitals in the Crimean Peninsula itself. This was a great shock to her, from which, it was said by some, she never really recovered and led to her becoming an invalid for many years. As she freely admitted to Sir John MacNeill, who was head of the Supplies Commission, illness at Scutari had been, 'generated within the building itself'. On first making this terrible discovery, that she and her nurses had not saved any lives at all, Florence Nightingale wanted, with commendable honesty, to publicize the fact at once. This did not suit anybody's interests. Florence Nightingale and her heroism had been one of the few good things to come out of the largely disastrous Crimean War and nobody, particularly in the government, wanted to see the nascent myth strangled almost at birth! She was persuaded to bury her findings among a more general report on army deaths.

Today, Florence Nightingale is remembered not for her patient and methodical analysis of mortality rates and other statistical information, but rather in the role of the little person standing up against authority, as personified by the senior army officers with whom she clashed. This makes a far more entertaining narrative than being elected a fellow of the Royal Statistical Society! That far from being a nobody, she was in fact the daughter of an extremely rich family and the personal friend of government ministers seldom comes into the story. Far better is the image of the little woman fighting all those crusty old men. It is this which has secured Nightingale's place in the hearts of the British, as somebody who stuck up for the ordinary soldiers and fought for their interests. No matter that what she was doing actually killed many of them.

The tragedy of Florence Nightingale's story is that here was a strong, capable and intelligent woman who undertook original work in a particular branch of mathematics, about which the average person knows nothing at all. She is destined to be recalled only as a saint-like character who wandered about the wards at night, carrying a lamp. It is not as an intelligent woman of action that she will forever be known, but rather what Longfellow called in his sentimental poem 'A noble type of good, Heroic womanhood.' This distorted image of one of the most remarkable women produced by nineteenth-century Britain is a sad epitaph, which means that Florence Nightingale's real and considerable achievements are never likely to be recognized.

Chapter 7

The Suffragettes 1903–1914:
'Votes for Ladies'

The opening ceremony of the 2012 Olympic Games in London was choreographed by Danny Boyle and watched in Britain by twenty-five million people. Hundreds of millions more watched it throughout the rest of the world. According to Danny Boyle, the whole thing had been inspired by one person, the suffragette Emily Davison, the middle-aged woman who died beneath the hoofs of the king's horse at the 1913 Derby. In one sequence of the extravaganza, Davison's death was re-enacted and she was shown being carried with her arms stretched out wide in a deliberate parody of Christian iconography. The audience were thus invited to compare her sacrifice with Christ's death on the cross. It is probably a reasonable assumption that not one person in a million watching this spectacle was aware that Emily Davison had been a terrorist bomber whose actions, far from helping hasten the granting of votes for women, actually delayed the process by several years.

There is in Britain a sentimental regard for the suffragettes, combined with an almost universally-held belief that they were responsible for the change in the law which granted the franchise to women. They are essentially seen as suffering martyrs, who used civil disobedience and generally peaceful means to draw attention to their cause. The chief image which we have of the suffragettes is that of patient women, enduring imprisonment and the horrors of hunger strikes and forced-feeding in pursuit of what is surely a just cause, that of equality of rights between men and women. The typical image of a suffragette may be seen in Illustration 13, which is a poster produced by the suffragettes and shows a lifeless woman lying in the jaws of a malevolent-looking cat. This woman is clearly a victim rather than an aggressor and it would be hard not to feel sympathy for her. The other famous picture of the suffragettes from that time is that of a woman being held down in a prison cell and force-fed by a villainous-looking man. This then is how we see the suffragettes today; trampled to death by a speeding horse, starving to death or being restrained in a prison cell.

The sentimental view of the suffragettes which has come down to us from that time was almost entirely a creation of the women themselves. In other words, we take them at their own evaluation; treating their propaganda posters as being objective, historical evidence. Even the slogan 'Votes for women', surely one of the most misleading political slogans ever devised, is treated as summing up the aims and purposes of the movement. To see what is wrong with the image that we now have of the suffragettes and their activities, it will be necessary to look at the real position of men and women when the violent agitation for female emancipation began during the Edwardian Era.

Three things are regarded as being almost axiomatic when considering the movement for the enfranchisement of women which was led by Emmeline Pankhurst and her suffragettes. The first is that men had the vote and women did not at that time, and secondly that the suffragettes were fighting so that all women might be able to vote. The third aspect of the case which is regarded as a self-evident truth is that the suffragettes somehow speeded up the process of women gaining the vote in Britain. All three beliefs are quite wrong.

The idea that men in Edwardian Britain had the vote and that women did not is such a strange one that it is, in retrospect, hard to know how it arose. Most probably, it is another example of subsequent generations taking suffragette propaganda at face value and not bothering to look at the facts behind the wild and intemperate rhetoric of the time.

The right to vote in the years before the First World War was dependent upon various things; including the ownership of property and having attended university. Following the Reform and Redistribution Acts of 1884–5, many men had still been left without the right to vote. When the suffragette agitation began in the early years of the twentieth century, about a third of men in England and Wales did not have the vote. In Scotland; the proportion of men without the right to vote was even higher. About 40 per cent of Scottish men could not vote. In Ireland, the situation was scandalous. Only half of all adult males in that part of the United Kingdom were entitled to vote in general elections. As if that was not bad enough, while some men had no vote, others had three! Until 1950, Oxford and Cambridge University both returned two MPs each to Parliament. Men who had attended these universities were therefore entitled to vote three times, twice for their university and once for their local constituency.

Strangely enough, those men who lacked the vote at that time were not particularly bothered about acquiring it. They were represented by the MP in whose constituency they lived anyway and most working men and women were more concerned about changing working conditions than they were about extending the franchise, which was a peculiarly middle-class obsession.

Many men did not have the vote in the years leading up to 1914, but a lot of women did. They could not, it was true, vote in general elections, but following the passage of the 1869 Municipal Franchise Act, women fulfilling certain property qualifications had been able to vote in local elections. In 1870, women had become eligible both to vote for, and also to serve on, the new School Boards. Five years later, women were given the right to be elected to serve as Poor Law Guardians and when County Councils were first established in 1888, women were also able to vote for them. In 1892, a major step forward for the enfranchisement of women was achieved, when it was ruled that women could be elected to serve on County Councils, the word 'man' in the relevant legislation being held also to include women.

By the turn of the century, 1,500 women in Britain held elected office, some as county councillors and others as poor law guardians or members of school boards. Without exception, these were well-educated and middle-class women who either owned property or had attended university. The position was therefore far more complex than many people suppose. An awful lot of working-class men were unable to vote at all, while many middle-class women were not only able to vote, but were also being elected to various roles in local government. All this had been achieved not by people throwing themselves under galloping horses or setting fire to pillar boxes, but rather by patient and tenacious women working relentlessly to change what they knew to be an unjust and inequitable political system.

Things had changed dramatically for women in the second half of the nineteenth century. We saw in the previous chapter that one of the reasons that Florence Nightingale was such a significant figure was not that she had saved any lives during the Crimean War, but rather because she made respectable the idea that women might work and achieve outside the purely domestic sphere of the home. This too had an effect on how people viewed the idea of women voting in Parliamentary elections. One of the traditional reasons that it was said women should not be allowed to vote was that their brains were in some way inferior to those of men and this would make it absurd for them to be given the responsibility of choosing a Member of Parliament. When women were admitted to universities in the late 1870s, it did not take long for this piece of nonsense to be proved false.

In 1887, a student called Aganata Ramsey was awarded a First Class Degree after taking the Cambridge classical tripos. As it happened, not a single male student at Cambridge that year achieved a first. So remarkable did this seem, that *Punch* magazine devoted a cartoon to Aganata Ramsey's accomplishment. Three years later, in 1890, Phillipa Fawcett came top in the mathematical tripos at Cambridge; beating all the men of her year. With women outperforming men intellectually, when once they had gained the opportunity to compete on level terms, there could be no longer be any excuse for silly talk about women's brains not being up to the job of voting in a general election.

In other fields too, women were breaking through old barriers and appearing in places which had previously been thought of as exclusively masculine domains. By 1911, there were 411 women doctors in Britain, with others qualifying as surgeons, dentists and architects. In 1913, the first female magistrate was appointed in London. In the first few years of the new century, it was plainly obvious to even the most diehard male reactionary that women were perfectly able to cope with both intellectual challenges and professional careers, every bit as well as any man. All the changes listed above had been achieved by patient and slow campaigning by women, with no violence or threats of disorder. Some of these same women were working in the early years of the twentieth century towards the granting of the vote to women in Parliamentary, as well as local elections, and there can be little doubt that they would have succeeded, had it not been for the eruption onto the scene of the suffragettes.

The women working to change the law on parliamentary elections were known as suffragists. In 1903, a new organization was founded by a woman called Emmeline Pankhurst. This was the Women's Social and Political Union. They wanted the vote at once, but only for university-educated women or those who owned property. They had no desire at all to see working-class women given the vote. For them, there was to be no quiet lobbying or discussions, they required a change in the law immediately and if they didn't get it, then things were likely to become unpleasant. It was these militant activists, those associated with the WSPU, who were in 1906 dubbed 'suffragettes' by the *Daily Mail*.

We have looked at, and shown to be false, the popularly-held notion that when the suffragettes began their violent campaign, men could vote and women could not, seeing that the actual state of affairs was immeasurably more complicated than that. We look next at another of the three misconceptions mentioned above, that the suffragettes were fighting for the granting of votes for all women. They were not. They were in fact perfectly happy to see the franchise restricted to middle and upper-class, property-owning women and those who had been educated at university. It was never their wish that working-class women should be given the vote. This sounds a controversial and revisionist view of history, but may easily be confirmed by simply looking at any of the literature which was being distributed by the Women's Social and Political Union, the official name of the suffragettes' organization. Printed clearly in the front of all their publications was the blunt and uncompromising statement that 'The Women's Social and Political Union are NOT asking for a vote for every woman'. This statement needs a little explanation.

There were two schools of thought about female enfranchisement in Britain, during the early part of the twentieth century. These were known as the 'universal' franchise and the 'equal' franchise. Those who supported the idea of the universal franchise believed that all adult men and women should be allowed to vote. Today, this seems to be the only fair way of arranging the electoral system. Those, like the suffragettes, who wanted equal franchise, on the other hand, were quite happy with the restricted right to vote, that was at that time based upon such qualifications as being a householder or having attended university. They just thought that well-off and well-educated women should be able to vote as well as men. This 'equal' franchise would have meant that a female factory owner would have been given the right to vote, but the women working for her, because they lived in rented accommodation, would not. One working-class woman, Ada Nield Chew, the daughter of a brick maker and who left school at the age of 11, summed the idea of the equal franchise up neatly: 'The entire class of wealthy women would be enfranchised . . . the great body of working women, married or single, would be voteless still.' Some people in the Labour Party, which was committed to a universal franchise, pointed out that rather than 'Votes for women', a more appropriate slogan for the suffragettes might have been, 'Votes for ladies', since it was upper middle-class ladies, rather than working-class women, who might benefit from their activities.

It is time to examine the influence that the Women's Social and Political Union, more commonly known as the suffragettes, had on the fight for the enfranchisement of women. Did they hasten or delay the granting of votes? What tactics did they use? And, even more importantly, whose interests did they represent, the ordinary working woman or the monied and propertied class to which most of the suffragette activists belonged themselves?

The impression one gets when reading about the suffragettes is that it was the struggle of powerless women with justifiable demands, who were being resisted by entrenched male chauvinists who were determined that women would never have the vote. This was not at all how things were. In fact there was almost unanimous agreement by most educated people and a majority of Members of Parliament that women should be enfranchised. The devil was, as is so often the case, in the details. In the 1890s 340 MPs, a sizeable majority, had pledged their support for female suffrage and in 1897, the House of Commons passed, with a majority of seventy-one, a motion calling for women to have the Parliamentary vote. The English-speaking world was moving in this direction and it would have been absurd for Britain to be left behind when everybody else was giving the vote to women.

The first place in the British Isles to allow women to vote also happened to be the location of the oldest continuously -operating parliament in the world. The Isle of Man, a self-governing British dependency in the Irish Sea, allowed women the vote in 1881. In 1893, New Zealand granted women the vote, including Maoris, and Australia soon followed suit. America had been even quicker off the mark: the state of Wyoming enfranchised women in 1869. By the turn of the century, a number of other states had also done so, among them Idaho, Utah and Colorado. The ridiculous state of affairs had there-fore arisen whereby a Maori woman in New Zealand had the Parliamentary vote, while women in London, the heart of the British Empire, did not. The enfranchisement of women soon became a worldwide trend.

In Europe, Finland granted the vote to women in 1906, followed by Norway in 1907. In 1915, Denmark enfranchised women, and in 1917 Canada, Russia, Poland, Latvia and Estonia did the same. The next year Germany, Hungary and Lithuania took this step and then in 1919, so did Austria, the Netherlands and South Rhodesia. In not one of these countries had there been any fuss or militant campaigning about the issue: it was just seen as the right and proper thing to do in a world which was changing and becoming more modern. Only in Britain had there been a huge fuss; impris-onment, hunger strikes, damage to property and so on.

In Edwardian Britain, it was not so much a question of *if* women were to be granted the vote, as *when* and on what terms. It is true that some men, including politicians, were not at all enthusiastic about the idea, but it was plain, because of developments throughout the world, that this was coming. The problem lay for the main political parties in seeing how much advantage they would be able to reap from female enfranchisement.

Perhaps a comparison with a modern-day situation relating to the British electoral system will make this a little easier to understand. There are, at the time of writing, plans to redraw the boundaries of Parliamentary constituencies, so as to make them all as nearly equal in size as possible.

As a result of this, a number of constituencies will be altogether abolished and the House of Commons will have fewer members. Now of course, the main political parties' views on this change are not shaped by abstract considerations of justice and equity. Rather, they wish to know if the boundary changes will rob them of the edge in the next general election. They wonder how many of their own MPs will be made redundant and what the implications might be if the next election is finely balanced. These are the sort of things which politicians worry about, not how fair this or that reform of the electoral system might be. So it was in the years before the First World War.

If the members of the Women's Social and Political Union had their way and women who fulfilled the same criteria as men were given the franchise, then this would give an immediate and marked advantage to the Conservatives. Well-to-do property owners were far less likely to vote for the Labour Party or Liberals. If, on the other hand, the universal franchise was adopted by the country, then not only would all women be able to vote, but in addition to that the third of men who were currently excluded from the electoral system would be able to vote too. Since these were mostly working-class people, living in rented accommodation, they would probably favour the Liberals and Labour at the ballot box. It was questions such as this which exercised the minds of the legislature, rather than high-minded notions of what was right. The only interest that most of those in Parliament had was how such a move would affect their own standing and chances of being returned at the next election. Some women fighting for the vote at that time realized all this and negotiated with politicians to try and thrash out a scheme which would satisfy everybody. Others, the members of the Women's Social and Political Union, broke windows, set fire to churches and planted bombs in public places.

Most people today are unaware of the ferocious campaign of bombing and arson carried out by the suffragettes in the years leading up to the outbreak of war in 1914. This is a pity, because without knowing what these extremists were up to, it is all but impossible to understand the attitude of the government towards them and, by extension, the whole question of female enfranchisement. It was these actions on the part of a tiny number of women which killed the whole question of electoral reform stone-dead and made it a certainty that women would not be granted the vote for the foreseeable future. Had it not been for the suffragettes, women would, almost without doubt, have been able to vote before, rather than after, the First World War.

The image of Emily Davison falling beneath a horse at the 1913 Derby is a powerful one. It was filmed by a newsreel camera, which ensured that an awful lot of people saw the incident and were affected by the ultimate sacrifice made for the cause of women's votes. What hardly anybody knows a century later though is that it was this woman who began the first terrorist campaign to take place in twentieth-century Britain. She began in a small way by setting fire to pillar boxes, but on 18 February 1913, Davison and other women planted a bomb in a house which Chancellor of the Exchequer David Lloyd George was having built at Walton in Surrey. At a little after six in the morning, the 5lbs of explosives went off, bringing down the ceilings and cracking a wall. The workmen were due just twenty minutes after the bomb went off and had they arrived just a little earlier, there could easily have been injuries or even fatalities. Emmeline Pankhurst had known about the planned bomb attack and she was arrested and charged with incitement. At the Old Bailey that April, Mrs Pankhurst was sent to prison for three years.

The activities of the suffragettes had already been making life difficult for those trying to reach a compromise with the government on the question of women's suffrage. Smashing windows and setting fire to buildings hardly helped to make the point that women were rational enough to be able to take part in the ordinary democratic process and when the explosions started, there was a hardening of positions on the part of Prime Minister Herbert Asquith's administration. It was simply impossible to give in to the threat of terrorism. Even those who had previously been supporters of the cause now moved to distance themselves from female enfranchisement.

It would take too long to list all the bombings carried out by the Women's Social and Political Union at this time and we must restrict ourselves to looking at some of the more notable. On 4 April, the day after Emmeline Pankhurst's trial ended, a bomb exploded at Oxted railway station in Surrey. A loaded pistol was found at the scene. On the afternoon of 14 April 1913, a bomb was planted outside the Bank of England. The fuse was burning and a very brave police officer carried it to a nearby fountain, extinguishing the fuse and preventing any casualties. Three days later, a bomb was placed outside Aberdeen railway station. It consisted of a large charge of gunpowder with a candle burning in it to act as a primitive fuse. A porter saw the device and put out the candle. On 24 April, a bomb exploded with devastating force at the headquarters of Northumberland County Council in Newcastle. Windows were shattered and the chimney of a neighbouring building blown down.

At the same time that these bombs were being planted, arson attacks were carried out, together with the sabotage of communications. On 9 March that same year, Saunderton and Croxley Green railway stations were destroyed by fire. Suffragette posters and literature were found nearby, including one which said, 'Women burning for the vote'. In Newcastle, telegraph poles were sawn down and telegraph wires were cut across England. Stately homes were also being torched.

The same day that the bomb exploded in Newcastle, another one caused extensive damage at the Free Trade Hall in Manchester. This was of significance to the suffragettes because it was here in 1905 that the first act of suffragette militancy took place, when Emmeline Pankhurst's daughter Christabel heckled Winston Churchill. Illustration 14 consists of newspaper headlines reporting some of these bomb attacks.

This is not a complete list of the attacks in April 1913, but gives some idea of the scale of the campaign being waged. Things were to get a good deal worse though, with bombs being planted across the whole of Britain and Ireland. The effects of the bombing, arson and sabotage could be clearly seen in the month following the burning of the railway stations and bombings in the north of England. A Liberal MP, Willoughby Dickinson, had introduced a private member's bill for women's suffrage, one which would have given women over the age of twenty-five who were either householders or married to householders the vote. In the past, such bills had always been given a second reading by a healthy majority and there was great optimism about this bill, because the Prime Minister had promised Dickinson that if his bill received a second reading, then the government would give it as much time as necessary to see that it became law.

On Wednesday, 7 May 1913, Willoughby Dickinson's bill was debated in the House of Commons. Foreign Secretary Edward Grey spoke in favour of it, but when the vote was taken on whether or not it should be given a second reading, 268 were against and only 221 in favour. It was a crushing defeat and the next day's newspapers had no doubt who was to blame for this. *The Times* carried an editorial which said;

> The band of women and girls who call themselves militant suffragettes have done their own cause more harm than they know. The embarrassment they have inflicted on their best friends has been growing more evident of late, and no attempt to conceal it was made in the House of Commons. It lay like a dead weight over the whole course of the debate on the bill.

In short, the best ever chance for passing a bill to enable women to have the vote had failed because so many Members of Parliament who had in the past supported female enfranchisement were horrified at the terrorism which was being conducted in the name of the cause. They felt that to align themselves with the Dickinson bill might make it appear that they countenanced the bombings.

It must also be borne in mind that Asquith's government was facing a number of threats, both on the domestic front and also the international scene, and could not afford to be seen as giving in to the threat of force. On the one hand, there had been terrible rioting less than two years earlier, in which troops had shot dead strikers. If the government appeared weak, it might act as an invitation for more unrest. Then again, Britain had almost gone to war with Germany in 1911 over the Agadir Crisis. There was an arms race between the two countries and it looked to many people as though Germany was watching Britain to see if the strength of purpose existed there to stand up against German actions in Europe or Africa. It was vital that the nations of Europe knew that the British government was resolute and determined not to be cowed by threats.

There was also the question of Ireland, which was at that time part of the United Kingdom. A civil war was brewing there between the Nationalists and those opposed to Home Rule. Both sides were arming themselves and the army could not be relied upon to maintain neutrality. This too was a desperately dangerous situation which could explode if people began to think that Asquith or his cabinet could be swayed by the threat or use of force. Talking of Ireland, it is interesting to recollect that the first terrorist bomb to explode in Northern Ireland during the twentieth century was planted not by the IRA but by the suffragettes at Lisburn's Christ Church Cathedral in 1914.

The defeat of the Dickinson Bill did nothing to discourage the members of the Women's Social and Political Union from the course upon which they had embarked. On the same day that it was voted down by the House of Commons, St Catherine's Church in Hatcham was burned to the ground. The suffragettes felt that the Church was a patriarchal institution and therefore a legitimate target for their attacks. On the morning of 7 May, a verger in St Paul's Cathedral heard an ominous ticking noise as he passed the bishop's throne. It was coming from a parcel which the police found to contain a time bomb. The explosive used in this was not gunpowder, but the far more powerful nitro-glycerine. Only a slight mechanical defect had prevented it from exploding.

For the next eighteen months, bombings and arson attacks took place across the whole of the United Kingdom. In May 1913, the Royal Observatory at Edinburgh was damaged by a bomb. The following month, bombs exploded at a new post office in Newcastle upon Tyne in the north of England, and also at Blackfriars Bridge in London. The day after the London attack, a large explosion damaged a canal bank in the Midlands. The intention had evidently been to flood surrounding low-lying farmland. Later in June, several stately homes in Scotland were burned down and on 5 July, there was an explosion at the Liverpool Cotton Exchange.

Ordinary people felt great anger towards the suffragette terrorists and meetings of the Women's Social and Political Union were sometimes disrupted by crowds hurling abuse at them for destroying churches and putting lives in danger. This too has become part of the mythology associated with the suffragettes. Photographs of furious men shouting references to bombings now appear misleadingly in books to illustrate how angry men were at the idea of women being allowed to vote! The longer that the terrorism continued, the further any sympathy that most people, men and women, felt for the suffragettes ebbed away.

On 11 November 1913, a bomb caused extensive damage to the greenhouse in Manchester's Alexandra Park. Three days later, a bomb was planted at the Sefton Park Palm House in Liverpool. On the night of Thursday, 18 December, the London districts of Camden and Holloway were rocked by the explosion of a charge of dynamite, which had been placed against the wall of Holloway Prison. Although only minor damage was caused to the prison, the windows of nearby houses were shattered and jagged shards of glass narrowly missed children asleep in their beds. It seemed to be a matter of time before people were killed by the reckless antics of the suffragettes. This happened less than a week later.

In April 1913, the police had raided the London headquarters of the Women's Social and Political Union. Among the documents seized was one which apparently came from a woman living on the south coast, who had a plan to attack a dockyard, causing a great deal of damage. Part of the letter read: 'Although I would love to be the sole villain of the piece, I fear the dockyard police would suspect a lady visitor, and so this time I propose to be the brains and not the hands. At any rate, the damage would be not less than £20,000.' The letter came from Hove and the nearest dockyard to there was Portsmouth. Causing such a large amount of harm to the place suggested that an arson attack was contemplated.

On the night of 20 December that year, a disastrous fire struck the Royal Dockyards at Portsmouth. It swept through some wooden buildings and spread to oil tanks. The battlecruiser *Queen Mary* was threatened by the flames and had to be towed to safety. The next day, the bodies of two sailors were found in the charred remains of the buildings where the fire had started. There had been so much fire-raising by the suffragettes that they were at once suspected of being behind the blaze in Portsmouth. Two days after the fire, the *New York Times* carried a headline which proclaimed that, '$1,000,000 damage and two deaths – suffragettes suspected'.

The fire in Portsmouth was never conclusively brought home to the suffragettes, although it was generally assumed that they had been behind it. Throughout the first eight months of 1914, bombings and arson attacks continued relentlessly. In Glasgow, a well-known glasshouse was wrecked by an explosion and churches in London were also bombed, including that of St Martin's-in-the-Fields at Trafalgar Square. On 11 June 1914, a bomb exploded in Westminster Abbey, which damaged stonework but caused no injuries. The following Saturday Philip Snowden, a Labour MP and firm supporter of female suffrage, gave a speech in which he said that: 'I totally disagree with the claim that militancy has advanced the cause. A year or so back there was the prospect of a measure passing the House of Commons, and I say now that through the action of a certain class, the suffrage question is as dead as Queen Anne.'

There was by now no Member of Parliament who would give any support to the cause of women gaining the vote. The day after Snowden's speech a bomb exploded in St George's Church in Hanover Square in the West End of London. The very last bomb of the terrorist campaign exploded in Northern Ireland at Lisburn's Christ Church cathedral. That same day, 1 August 1914, Germany declared war on Russia and then, two days later, on France. The First World War had begun. With the outbreak of war, the suffragettes announced a truce and threw themselves into the war effort. At the end of hostilities in 1918, some women were given the vote in Britain; just as they were in other countries at that time. The militancy had been at best useless and at worst actually counter-productive.

Why are Emily Davison and the Pankhursts remembered now with such fondness, since their efforts were ultimately fruitless? The answer is that, like Florence Nightingale, they epitomize the little person fighting against great odds for a noble cause. These were ordinary women who squared up to the Prime Minister and his reactionary colleagues and, according to the myth, triumphed in the end. The cause for which they were fighting was so manifestly justified and right, that there is a tendency to overlook the actual effect on that cause of the methods used by its wilder supporters. That a handful of dedicated women could, by hunger strikes, smashing windows and hurling themselves beneath galloping horses, have altered the entire political structure of Britain seems to us a century later as a remarkable achievement. It would not make nearly so satisfying a story if we acknowledged that these same women were ruthless terrorists, quite prepared to take innocent lives in pursuit of their cause.

The suffragettes were a product of the Edwardian society and theirs is but one strand in the turbulent history of that period of British history. The Edwardian years, from 1901 to 1914, justify close examination because they shed light on yet another common theme in the British psyche; the desire to hark back to a mythical and non-existent golden age. This is an idea which we shall explore in the next chapter.

Chapter 8

The Golden Age of Edwardian Britain 1901–1914: 'La Belle Epoque'

It is time to look at a period in Britain's history which may seem eerily familiar to modern readers. It was a time when a Home Secretary stood up in the House of Commons and admitted that there had, in the last twelve months, been a net migration to this country of 600,000 people. Most of these newcomers were seeking refuge from supposed persecution, who we would today call 'asylum seekers'. He also discussed the possibility that some people were coming to this country for the sole purpose of seeking medical treatment, which today we know as 'health tourism', and went on to talk of 'people smugglers'. It was a time when another MP complained that at some schools in his constituency, 'Few English pupils are to be found'. He claimed that there was a housing crisis, caused by immigration. The debates on this subject in Parliament were in response to a deep unease felt by ordinary people about mass immigration. There was particular concern that the influx of unskilled workers from Eastern Europe was driving down wages and making it harder for British workers to find jobs. A far-right group called the British Brotherhood was founded. Their slogan was, 'England for the English'.

The crisis over immigration at that time, which was running at levels which dwarf anything seen today, was compounded by the fear of separate societies developing, communities where many people did not even speak English. It was thought that not only were all these foreigners taking jobs away from the British, but that fanatical terrorists were being sheltered within such communities and that bombings and shootings were taking place as a direct consequence of allowing so many foreigners, with ideas so different from those traditionally held in Britain, to flood the country. As if that were not enough, tensions within society caused a series of strikes and outbreaks of ferocious rioting, one hot summer, so widespread and violent that the police were unable to cope. These problems were all being exacerbated by a revolution in information technology, which mean that people were learning far more rapidly than ever before about what was going on in other parts of the country.

All this sounds uncannily like the kind of problems with which we are currently wrestling and it is hard to believe that we are talking of the Edwardian Era, over a hundred years ago. Mass immigration, terrorism, rioting, political crises, industrial unrest, all fuelled and encouraged by an information revolution; these are the themes at which we shall be looking in this chapter.

The idea that there once was a golden age, when everything was a lot better than it is today, has been popular for at thousands of years. Sometimes, the supposed golden age is thought to have been centuries ago. We saw an example of this in Chapter 1 with the Victorian interest in the Medieval and Gothic. For some artists and poets at that time, the fourteenth century was manifestly a better era than their own. There has in this country, for over a century now, been an enduring belief in one particular golden age which is still thought by many people to have been a special time; a brief era when everything was going well, at least for Britain and the British. This is the Edwardian period, which is usually considered to have lasted from Queen Victoria's death in 1901 to the outbreak of the First World War in the summer of 1914. Calling these years the 'Edwardian' period is something of a misnomer of course, for Edward VII, after whom the era was named, actually died in 1910. Nevertheless, most historians consider that 1914 marks the end of the Edwardian Era.

The expression 'Victorian' can have negative connotations and may even be used in a pejorative sense as being synonymous with 'Dickensian'. When we talk of 'Victorian' working conditions, we are calling to mind Oliver Twist and workhouses. 'Edwardian', on the other hand, has quite another meaning; the word is redolent of opulence, wealth and elegance. Those thirteen years of the Edwardian period are often thought to have been the high-water mark of empire, a time when Britain's influence upon the world was at its zenith and the country was enjoying the fruits of the mightiest empire which the world had ever seen, one which covered a quarter of the earth's land surface and included a fifth of the world's population. The Boer War had just ended and Britain was to be at peace for the whole of those thirteen years. It was a time of new technology and increasing standards of living. Prosperity at home and power abroad are what the Edwardians are known for. It was the age of Elgar and Kipling, a time of certainty about Britain and its values. In later years, it would become customary to speak wistfully of the years 'before the war' when everything had been so much better, in so many ways.

It was not until after the First World War, however, that the early years of the twentieth century began to be viewed with such nostalgia. It was then that a term was coined for the late Victorian and Edwardian period in Western Europe. The expression chosen to define this period was 'La Belle Epoque', which translates roughly as 'the beautiful era'. The poet Wordsworth wrote that 'distance lends enchantment to the view' and nowhere is the truth of this sentiment better illustrated than in the view of Edwardian Britain; which became increasingly enchanting the further the distance in time which separated it from observers grew. Within twenty years of the end of that epoch, the false view of the pre-war years had become firmly established and a new golden age existed as the focus for the nostalgia of those who really ought to have known better.

Illustration 15 shows the kind of visual image which the word 'Edwardian' evokes for many of us. It shows grandly-dressed ladies at Ascot in 1905. Sunny days such as this, with people dressed up for Henley or Ascot sum up Edwardian Britain – a never-ending summer, where everything is right in the world and Britain enjoys its rightful place in the world. No more pressing concern than which lacy parasol to choose that day. The reality though, could hardly be more different.

In recent years, the Western World has gone through what is sometimes referred to as the 'Digital Revolution'. The after-effects of this technological upheaval are still being felt and it has not yet ended. Mechanical household gadgets with which we have been familiar for many decades have all been swept away: the typewriters and cameras, telephones and radios, record players and tape recorders, all have been consigned to the dustbin of history. This rapid process has changed British society in many ways and had a dramatic affect in many ways upon how we run our lives. Much the same thing was happening in Edwardian Britain, but this revolution was an analogue, rather than a digital, one. It added to the feeling among ordinary people that the world was changing more rapidly than ever before and that nobody quite knew what would happen next.

Britain has changed greatly in the last twenty years or so for other reasons, beside the introduction of amazing new ways of communicating with other people and handling information. Mass immigration has altered the face of the larger cities irrevocably and the spectre of terrorism has, at the same time, grown to be an ever-present fear. These two things, immigration and terrorism, are often connected in people's minds, because most of the terrorism which occurs in Britain seems to be carried out by people whose origins lie outside the country. This too would have been an idea familiar to

the Edwardians. We begin our survey of the Edwardian 'golden age' by looking at the way in which the people of that time saw their country changing
and the uneasiness which this occasioned in some citizens.

In twenty-first century Britain, anxieties about immigration and terrorism often centre around Muslims. It is feared that many of them owe their
first allegiance not to Britain, but to an unfamiliar religion which causes
them to think and act in very different ways from most British people.
Combined with this is a supposed propensity among some Muslims for violence and terrorism. However irrational these feelings might be; they are
certainly held by a large section of the population. A century earlier, the
fear was of Eastern Europeans, especially Jews, and the way in which they
flooded the country and occupied swathes of what we now refer to as the
'inner cities'. They spoke other languages, either followed a strange religion
or were atheists, and ate unfamiliar foods. This led to a tendency to form
parallel societies and embrace dangerous political ideologies; some of which
led to violence. They certainly didn't subscribe to what we now call 'British
Values'.

Perhaps one or two specific instances of the way in which the events in
Edwardian society and the fears that such things generated precisely mirror
what is going on in Britain today will make this easier to understand. In 2005,
an armed robbery in Bradford was bungled disastrously and a police officer,
Sharon Beshenivsky, was shot dead. The crime was carried out by asylum
seekers and some people drew conclusions from this about the wisdom of
allowing large numbers of such people to enter the country and remain here
as long as they pleased. That the killer was a Muslim did not help matters.
There was a general feeling that this was a uniquely horrible crime which
was symptomatic of modern society. Surely, this kind of thing didn't used to
happen in the old days?

On Saturday, 23 January 1909, a crime almost identical to the murder of
Sharon Beshenivsky took place in the north London suburb of Tottenham.
Tottenham is today known as an area with many ethnic minorities, not a few
of whom are asylum seekers. The situation was no different a century ago,
except that at that time, most of the asylum-seekers were from Poland and
Russia and many of them were Jews. In fact before the First World War, one
part of Tottenham was known as 'Little Russia', due to the large number of
Russians who had settled there. The area had a number of synagogues.

On that Saturday morning in 1909, Schnurmann's rubber factory in
Chesnut Road, just off the high road, was just about to stop work for the
weekend. Saturday was payday and a car arrived from a nearby bank with

the wages. No sooner had the clerk got out of the car, than two men rushed up, knocked him down and made off with the bag containing £80. Some of the workers from the factory, angry at the prospect of being deprived of their money, gave chase. At the corner of the street, the two robbers turned and opened fire with automatic pistols, wounding one man and sending the others diving for cover.

The sound of gunfire brought three police officers running from nearby Tottenham Police Station. The gunmen opened fire at them and the three men sheltered behind a wall. At this point, a ten-year-old boy called Ralph Joscelyn ran out of his house to see what was going on. He was promptly shot dead. The bandits hoped to escape across the open country which surrounded Tottenham at that time and they made off across the fields towards Walthamstow. Some of the policemen from the police station followed them, while others broke out the revolvers which were kept there. Incredibly, there were also in the armoury cutlasses, which were at one time standard issue to the police in Britain. These too were handed out and some officers then set off on bicycles, waving swords. It might have been comic if not for the deadly serious threat faced by both the police and civilians caught up in the affair.

The first police officer to catch up with the men who had carried out the wages snatch was PC William Tyler. He was shot dead. There then followed a long chase, in which the bandits exchanged shots with not only the pursuing police, but also several farmers armed with shotguns. At one point, a tram was hijacked and then, when they could flee no more, the two men shot themselves.

The men who had carried out the robbery which went so disastrously wrong were both Eastern European asylum-seekers, Jewish anarchists who had been allowed to settle in Britain. Their names were Paul Hefeld and Jacob Lepidus. They had been trying to raise funds to finance revolutionary activity in their home countries on the Baltic Sea, which were at that time part of the Russian Empire. The funerals of PC Tyler and little Ralph Joscelyn were held together on the same day and some 50,000 people lined the route of the funeral corteges. There was already a lot of anti-Semitism in the country and the fact that both the killers were Jewish refugees exacerbated this. That they were also anarchists did not help either.

Today, there is a general lack of understanding in Britain of an ideology which causes men to sacrifice their lives in suicide bombings. We view such actions as quite mad. Since the people who carry out these crimes are invariably Muslims, there is an association in the minds of many ordinary British people with the idea of Islam and ruthless murders carried out without any regard for the lives of the perpetrators. Much the same was thought about Jews and anarchism in the early part of the twentieth century. Bombings, shootings and assassinations were being carried out across Europe by men who seemingly did not care if they sacrificed their own lives in the process. As far as could be understood, these dangerous fanatics were opposed to our very way of life and once settled in Britain would not hesitate to carry on with their conspiracies and terrorist campaigns. The resonance between this situation and the state of affairs in modern Britain is strong.

The popular feeling after what became known as the 'Tottenham Outrage' was that these murderous terrorists had been sheltered in a community which had been given refuge in the country, and had allowed these men to live among them. It was not precisely a rational viewpoint, but we see similar sentiments after crimes by asylum-seekers in Britain today.

The year after the Tottenham Outrage, there was an even more brutal crime involving the murder of police officers by Jewish anarchists. On the night of 16 December 1910, a group of foreign terrorists living in the East End of London were disturbed by the police while in the process of burgling a jeweller's shop. The unarmed officers were gunned down, two sergeants and a constable being killed. There had been nothing like this before in Britain and three police officers would not be killed simultaneously in this way again until the Shepherds Bush murders in 1966.

The aftermath of what became known, due to the location of the crime, as the Houndsditch Murders became headline news across the world. Two weeks after the killing of the police officers, a tip-off led to a house in London's East End, where the killers were said to be hiding out. When the police knocked on the door of the nondescript house in Stepney, they were met by a hail of gunfire and swiftly retreated. The house, 100 Sidney Street, was surrounded by the police and the famous Siege of Sidney Street had begun.

The only firearms to which the police had access, shotguns and old revolvers, were hopelessly inadequate for an operation of this sort. The men in the upper stories of the house in Sidney Street were armed with modern semi-automatic pistols, German Mausers whose magazines meant that they were able to maintain a constant and withering fire against the men surrounding their hideout. The police were forced to move back to the end of the street and found themselves quite at a loss to know how to proceed.

The Home Secretary at the time was Winston Churchill and, as a former soldier, he naturally favoured a military solution. Churchill was in the bath when news was relayed to him of the gun battle which was raging in East London. He dressed and immediately authorized the use of troops to tackle this unprecedented situation. Soldiers of the Scots Guards, stationed at the Tower of London, were sent for. The Home Secretary made the most injudicious decision to go to Sidney Street and direct operations himself, something for which he was later ridiculed in the House of Commons. When he got to the scene, Churchill was greeted by the crowds gathered there with catcalls and cries of 'Who let them in?', a reference to the widespread belief that there was unchecked immigration into Britain and that this gun battle was a natural consequence of what we now call 'porous borders'.

The soldiers who arrived to aid the police soon set up positions and began exchanging fire with the cornered terrorists. In a decided case of overkill, Churchill had also arranged for a troop of horse artillery to come to Stepney, the intention being to shell the street in order to subdue the two or three desperate criminals who were trapped in one house. In the event, field guns were not needed, because the house caught fire and the charred corpses of two men were found in the ruins.

It is in the sequel to this famous incident that the similarities with our own time become very obvious. Today, news of even the most trifling incident will be spread across the country, indeed the world, quite literally at the speed of light. Electronic media mean that images from the scene of a riot or terrorist attack begin circulating almost immediately. This marvel is achieved by the use of digital technology; something which has had the most profound effect on how we see and interpret current affairs. The Edwardian period was on the cusp of another sort of information revolution, one which had an equally great impact on society at that time.

Digital technology works by reducing information about photographs, films, text, music and the spoken word to a string of binary digits, in which form it may readily be transmitted along telephone lines or on radio waves to a destination anywhere in the world. Once there, it is reassembled into a coherent form which we understand. The predecessor to digital information was analogue technology, whereby an image or piece of text is simply copied and the copy sent, just as it is, to somewhere else. A traditional photograph is a representation, or analogue, of the actual scene at which the camera lens has been pointed.

In the nineteenth century, during the reign of Queen Victoria, the creation and distribution of photographs and printed material was slow, laborious and expensive; it hardly affected ordinary people. Newspapers, the commonest means of presenting information about current affairs, were too pricy for the working man or woman to think of buying and they seldom contained photographs. A riot or terrorist bombing in Manchester during the 1860s would only slowly, over a period of weeks, become known to the man in the street and then almost invariably by word of mouth, rather than by reading about it or seeing pictures taken at the scene. This meant of course that in Victorian Britain, accurate and up-to-date information was not a common commodity. All this was to change in the decade or so following Queen Victoria's death in 1901.

The rise of photographic film made from celluloid rather than glass plates and the advent of cheap newspapers changed all this during the years before the First World War. The arrival too of moving pictures made a huge difference to the way that working people in Britain thought about their way of life and the social order. The ha'penny newspapers such as the *Daily Mail*, the *Sketch* and the *Daily Mirror* became tremendously popular and each copy was passed around in public houses and so on. For the first time in British history, the ordinary men and women of the country could read about, look at photographs of and even see moving images of events which they would never be likely to see in real life. For many, this was a revelation with far-reaching implications. The 'Siege of Sidney Street', for example, was filmed and the images shown at thousands of music halls and theatres across the whole of the United Kingdom.

By 1912 there were an estimated 4,000 cinemas in Britain and almost all of them showed newsreel films as well as the main programme. In music halls too, a very important part of working-class culture at that time, the programme often ended with a newsreel produced by the Biograph company, for instance. The majority of working people in the country would therefore have seen Pathé newsreels of things such as the affair at Sidney Street and other dramatic incidents like the suffragette Emily Davison throwing herself under the horses at the 1913 Derby.

It was not of course only dramatic events such as terrorist attacks or spectacular suicides which were being read about in the new, cheap newspapers or watched in newsreels by working people. The lives of the wealthy and famous were also featured, events such as Henley Regatta, the well-to-do at Ascot, the Oxford and Cambridge boat race, Royal visits and many other news items which showed the enormous gulf which existed between the rich and poor of Britain. This could not but have the effect of drawing the attention of working-class people at the music hall to the unbelievably ostentatious way of life enjoyed by those above them on the social scale. These constant reminders of their lowly status in the established order of things was manifested in the rise of support for socialism and the trade union movement. The increased support for trade union militancy, fuelled by a new awareness of, and anger about, the inequalities in Edwardian society led to what became known as the 'Great Unrest'. This was a series of strikes and demonstrations which culminated in the most ferocious and deadly rioting ever seen in mainland Britain.

We tend all too often to take our view of Edwardian Britain from fiction, rather than fact. Television programmes such as *Upstairs, Downstairs* or *Downton Abbey* are treated as factual accounts of this period of history. Sometimes, we have a vague idea about Edwardian London from watching films like *Mary Poppins,* with the visually attractive and stable life of the upper middle classes shown as the norm. Even the lives of working men such as Bert the chimney sweep in *Mary Poppins* are seen as being one long round of gaiety and larks. The reality was very different. The years leading up to the outbreak of war in 1914 were times of great hardship for many workers. There was rising unemployment, with no social security benefits to cushion the impact. Men, women and children were literally starving to death. It was to stave off the rising tide of anger from the ordinary population that the Liberal government of the time instituted measure such as Old Age Pensions and embarked upon a scheme aimed at redistributing the nation's wealth. The effect upon somebody whose neighbours were literally dying of hunger of seeing a newsreel of grand folk at the Henley Regatta can only be imagined!

Between 1910 and 1912, prices of goods in the shops, as well as rents, rose inexorably. At the same time, wages fell in real terms. This produced a feeling of despair, the practical expression of which was a wave of strikes for increases in pay which grew to a crescendo in 1911. Dockers and railway workers were among those involved in these industrial disputes, which meant that imported food was left rotting by the dockside and that which did get through the docks could not be transported to other parts of the country. These labour troubles rumbled on until the summer and then exploded into violence. Matters were not helped by the weather that year.

It is a matter of common observation that rioting and disorder tends to be more frequent in hot, sunny weather than when it is cold, rainy and overcast. The summer of 1911 was gloriously sunny from May until September. In July a temperature of 96.8 degrees Fahrenheit was recorded at Ascot and that month still holds the record for the amount of sunshine seen in one month in this country, a total of 384 hours at the south coast resort of Worthing. The heat however, welcome as it was for holidaymakers, had a bad effect upon the crowds of angry and discontented workers who were striking that summer. The industrial areas of Britain were a tinder box.

The hot weather coincided with a series of major strikes. In May, dock workers went on strike for better working conditions and an increase in wages. By August, 20,000 dockers had walked out in London and in Liverpool the docks had been brought to a complete standstill. Some carters also came out on strike, which meant that raw materials could not be transported to and from the docks. There was mass picketing and violent scenes in London, with lorries and buses overturned by angry crowds of strikers. On 11 August, the government made the fateful decision to use troops to restore order and ensure that supplies began moving again. The carters ended their strike that day, but now it was the turn of the railwaymen to take industrial action.

A century ago, the railways were the arteries of Britain. They were the only the way of getting from one end of the country to the other and no government could allow its trade and industry to be paralysed by a union in this way. Troops were sent into London and Liverpool to protect the railway lines from sabotage and ensure that those who wished to continue driving trains were not prevented from doing so by intimidation from union pickets. Over 12,000 soldiers were quartered in London and Hyde Park was turned into a tented army camp. Troops with fixed bayonets guarded the main railway stations and patrolled the lines. In Liverpool, 3,500 soldiers were brought in to prevent disorder, but their presence in the city had precisely the opposite effect.

Almost a quarter of a million men and women were on strike in Liverpool by 13 August and a strike committee was now virtually running the city, deciding which vehicles could use the streets and who might and might not work. It looked very much like a parallel government along the line of the soviets which emerged during the Russian Revolution a few years later, and when a crowd of 80,000 men gathered and began moving towards the centre of the city, it was felt that firm action was needed. A large body of police was formed to break up the march and they were backed by cavalry. After the Riot Act had been read by a magistrate, anybody who remained on the streets was defying the law and force could legitimately be used to disperse any gathering. The mounted troops then attempted to clear the streets, with disastrous consequences.

Before the reading of the Riot Act, the demonstration had been peaceful, if a little boisterous. When the police moved in and began to push people back and the cavalry began riding into groups of strikers, violence erupted. Almost 200 strikers were hospitalized with injuries caused by the heavy-handed tactics used against them by the troops and police. Windows were smashed, fires started and makeshift barricades set up to block the streets. A hundred or so men and a few women were arrested and taken to court the following day on charges ranging from obstruction to assaulting the police. The stage was now set for the final act of the tragedy.

A warship, the cruiser HMS *Antrim*, had been ordered to Liverpool and was anchored in the Mersey. Armed sailors landed and took control of the docks, while heavily-armed troops patrolled the streets in a bid to deter further gatherings of strikers. Police in armoured cars were also in evidence. Illustration 16 shows a line of troops, behind which is a police armoured car. This is not the usual sort of thing which we think of when Edwardian Britain is mentioned! The stage was set for the final act of the tragedy.

The members of the crowd who had been arrested appeared in court on 15 August and were, almost without exception, either sentenced immediately to prison or remanded in custody to face trial at a later date on more serious charges. The vans carrying the prisoners to Walton Prison had been assigned a guard of thirty hussars, mounted soldiers carrying rifles. The relatives and friends of the men being taken off to prison had formed a sizable and hostile crowd in the streets between the court and the prison and were blocking the way forward for the prison vans. Then, bottles and stones began to be thrown at the cavalry escort. It was unclear if this was an attempt to rescue the prisoners by breaking open the vans, but whatever the intention, it could have come as little or no surprise when things grew very ugly.

The vans and their military escort were now hemmed in on all sides and unable to move forward or back. Some of the men in the crowd now darted forward and grabbed at the bridles of the soldiers' horses, perhaps trying to move them away from the vans. At this point, the order was given to open fire and the hussars levelled their rifles at the crowd and began shooting. Five men were hit by the hail of fire, two of whom died almost at once. John Sutcliff was shot twice in the head. He and Michael Prendegast, the other fatality, were both in their twenties. The sudden, shocking death of these two young men, both were in their twenties, seemed to bring the city of Liverpool to its senses. Before the railway strike ended though, there was to be even more bloodshed elsewhere in the country.

Incredibly, the two deaths in Liverpool were not the worst loss of life in the disturbances which racked Britain that summer. Things were even worse in South Wales. In the mining districts, feelings were running very strongly against the authorities and there was great support for the striking railwaymen. Some engine drivers though resisted the call to strike and trains still ran. One reason that it was so important to the government that the railways kept running was that it was by means of the railways that troops were moved from one part of the country to another. Over 50,000 soldiers had been mobilized and the railway system was vital for transporting them to where they were needed. In addition to the other problems facing the government at that time, a civil war was looking increasingly likely in Ireland and it was necessary to move military reinforcements to ports in Wales, so that they could take ship for Ireland. The Great Western line, for instance, ran through South Wales to Fishguard and was a quick route to move men and equipment to the restive southern provinces of Ireland.

The railway line to the Welsh ports in the south ran through Llanelli and the strikers there and their supporters were utterly determined that there would be no strike-breaking in the area. Trouble erupted on 18 August, when hundreds of men, including not only strikers but also colliers and tinplate workers who supported the railwaymen, blocked two level crossings on the line through Llanelli. A local magistrate appealed for military assistance, as the police were unable to clear the tracks. The following day, troops from the Worcestershire Regiment arrived in Llanelli, with orders to secure the railway line and ensure that trains could pass freely through the district. When attempts were made to prevent a passenger train from advancing to the coast, the troops were given the order to fix bayonets and charge the crowd. They did so, but as the train entered a steep cutting, some of the strikers climbed onto the locomotive and raked out the fire. This meant that the line between England and the South Wales ports was now completely closed. Soldiers who had followed the men intent upon sabotaging the train now found themselves trapped in the cutting and the crowd showed their feelings by throwing stones and lumps of coal down at them from the embankments.

The situation for the surrounded troops was embarrassing, rather than dangerous and the obvious solution would have been for their officer to order them to retreat. As it was, he gave the order to open fire. Two men were killed in the first volley. This was the signal for some of the most ferocious rioting to be seen in Britain that year. Over the next few hours, trains were set on fire and looted, with terrible consequences. One wagon in a railway siding was full of calcium carbide, an explosive chemical. When this was torched, there was a tremendous blast, which killed four men.

The railway strike was settled by a combination of concessions which the companies running the lines were encouraged to make by the government and also, supposedly, by appeals to the patriotism of the strikers. The Agadir Crisis in July had nearly ended in war between Britain and Germany and the railways would have been crucial in mobilizing the army. The leaders of the strike were asked if they really wished to cripple the army, in the event of a war. This at least was the public perception of the resolution to some of the most violent and damaging industrial action ever see in Britain. There was another reason why the railway companies were urged to settle and end the strike. Having chosen to use the armed forces to confront the workers and prevent what could end up as a general strike, it was essential that troops could be moved swiftly to where they were needed in Britain; whether Liverpool, London or Llanelli. With the railway network more or less in the hands of the strikers, the very movement of the troops was under the control of the men facing them. It was, as the strike continued, becoming almost impossible for the government in London to be sure of transporting soldiers to where they were most needed. Home Secretary Winston Churchill summed the matter up in his usual, pithy manner, declaring, 'We cannot keep the trains running. There is nothing we can do. We are done!'

A few years later, in 1914, David Lloyd George revealed that even without the use of railways, Winston Churchill had thought that the government could still defeat the rebellious strikers in Wales. The account which Lloyd George gave of the crisis shows more clearly than anything, just how fragile was the stability of Edwardian Britain and how close it really was to the abyss of what was practically civil war. Writing of the summer of 1911, he said that:

> Winston then had a plan to shut the Welsh miners into their valleys by a military cordon and to starve them out. A mad plan. He had all the country planned out for a military campaign. I shall never forget the remarkable scene which I witnessed at the Home Office. Winston with his generals, and his plan of campaign.

Fortunately, wiser counsels than Churchill's won the day and the plan for what would have amounted to a war was quietly abandoned.

In Wales though, there was to be still more disorder which would need to be put down by the army, even with the end of the railway strike. We saw earlier in this chapter that there was considerable unease about the scale of immigration into Britain in the first years of the twentieth century. Some of this popular discontent was linked to anti-Semitism, a large number of the refugees being Jewish. As is still the case today, most of the asylum seekers sought to stay in London and the other large cities, the places where there were already communities of people from the same countries as those from which they had fled. There was also more opportunity for work in the cities. Some though found their way to South Wales, where they mostly set up as small shopkeepers.

The newsreels of the 'Battle of Stepney', as the Siege of Sidney Street was also known, had been shown at cinemas and music halls across the whole country and the scenes of soldiers engaging in a gun battle with foreign Jews brought out the worst instincts in some people. There was general anger not only about the danger posed by allowing so many asylum-seekers into Britain, people who would willingly shelter terrorists, but also against Jews in general. This led to the first pogroms in Britain since the Middle Ages.

The railway strike had been settled on 19 August, but there was still unrest and it was not long before a new target for the angry working men of South Wales was found. Tredegar was a town containing 20,000 people. Of these, only thirty families were Jews. The rumour began to be spread that these Jews monopolized the shops and other businesses in the town. There were in fact just seventeen Jewish shopkeepers in Tredegar, along with a rabbi and one or two other businessmen. No sooner had the strike ended and the troops returned to their barracks, than rioting began in Tredegar, with the aim of driving out all the Jews living there. Shops were besieged and looted, the police being unable to cope with this new outburst of violence.

From Tredegar, the anti-Jewish rioting spread to Ebbw Vale, Brynmawr, Bargoed and several other villages and towns. The single avowed aim of those taking part in these disturbances was to drive all the Jews from South Wales. In Ebbw Vale, a tobacconist's shop owned by a Jew was surrounded and then broken into and looted. The owner and his family retreated upstairs to their living quarters and then barricaded themselves into the attic. Even the floor-boards were ripped up and the light fittings pulled from the walls, so as to render the place uninhabitable.

The police in Wales were quite unable to cope with the mounting disorder in the valleys of South Wales and, for the second time that month, the decision was made to call for the army to come to the aid of the civil power. Elements of the Somerset Light Infantry and Worcestershire Regiment were brought into Tredegar and other towns. It took some determined efforts, even for the troops, to bring the situation under control and bayonet charges were made along the streets, before the rioters realized that there was to be no more pussy-footing around. A number of Jewish families were evacuated from the area, leaving behind their wrecked homes. It was one of the most shameful episodes in twentieth-century British history, a pogrom indistinguishable from those taking place at that time in Tsarist Russia.

The events which we have been examining in this chapter do not really give the appearance of any kind of 'golden age'. The Edwardian period instead looks very much like our own, with many of the same problems with which are all too familiar today. It is fascinating though to see how modern politicians talk about this kind of thing now, as though nothing like that used to happen in the old days. After the rioting in the summer of 2011, the Prime Minister at the time, David Cameron, gave a speech in which he outlined the thesis that Britain was, in some obscure way, 'broken'. Cameron went on to detail just how this state of affairs had arisen, explicitly stating that it was a relatively recent development and that this sort of thing wouldn't have happened in the good old days. In adopting this line, the Prime Minister was making a quite conscious and deliberate attempt to present a rose-tinted image of the past, a time when rioting youths would not have been tolerated. He said:

> So this must be a wakeup call for our country. Social problems that have been festering for decades have exploded in our face . . . Do we have the determination to confront the slow-motion moral collapse that has taken place in parts of our country these past few generations? . . . Children without fathers. Schools without discipline. Reward without effort. Crime without punishment.

It will be observed that the problems which caused the rioting are apparently relatively recent: only a few decades or generations ago, things were quite different in this country. It is soft teachers in schools, single-parent families and courts that are not strict enough which have brought about the crisis; contributing to, or even causing, 'broken Britain'. Things were, we are given to understand, very different in the past, when children had fathers, schools had discipline and crimes were punished. This is either shameless dishonesty on an industrial scale, or abysmal ignorance. When making these references to a lost golden age of stability and order, did Cameron really not know about the waves of rioting which have regularly swept Britain for the whole of its history? Instead of moaning about 'broken Britain', he should have been counting himself lucky that it had not been necessary, as it had been for a British Prime Minister a century earlier, to mobilize the army and navy to tackle the disorder!

Even odder was the expressed opinion of David Lammy, the MP for Tottenham, where the rioting had begun. Mr Lammy thought that a contributory factor in the riots had been the Labour government's decision in 2004 to tighten up the law around corporal punishment given to children by their parents. He said in an interview, 'Many of my constituents came up to me after the riots and blamed the Labour government, saying, "You guys stopped us being able to smack our children."' Apparently, the MP, who smacked his own small children, tended to agree that a lack of corporal punishment had led to young people getting out of control.

We see in the views of both the former Prime Minister and also an MP who was at one time an Education Minister, a yearning for a vanished past, where parents, especially fathers judging by what Mr Cameron said, kept order and disciplined their children so that they would not end up as hooligans. It is unclear from what Cameron said, precisely when this golden age of well-behaved children and tough schools and courts actually was. Presumably the time of his own childhood, three or four decades earlier. The yearning for a vanished golden age of stability an order is a persistent one and manifests itself in various ways down the years. Edwardian Britain has lingered on as an idealised version of this fantasy.

After the dreadful events of 1911, there may have been those who hoped that life in Britain would improve, but they were destined to be disappointed. Industrial unrest soared in the following years. In 1911, a total of ten million working days were lost due to strike action. The following year, this had risen to forty million days lost. Not only that, but the country was slowly but inexorably slipping towards civil war. At that time, Ireland was an integral part of the United Kingdom and yet the government was planning to introduce a measure of Home Rule. This was being vociferously opposed by many politicians and senior army officers. Protestants in the north of Ireland were preparing to fight against any Home Rule and were, with this end in mind, smuggling arms into the country. The intention was to set up a provisional government in Belfast. Nationalists too were running guns into the country and it was not clear if the army would obey orders to tackle the Unionists in Ulster or if they would instead side with them.

The very real chance that a civil war would break out in Britain and that the army would lack the resolve necessary to tackle it was a terrifying one for the government of the day. There seemed no way out of the crisis until the same *Deus ex machina* as the one which resolved the struggle with the suffragettes intervened and rescued Prime Minister Herbert Asquith. War broke out in the summer of 1914, just as it seemed as though fighting was about to start in Ireland for control of the country. The resultant surge of patriotism postponed the day of reckoning for a few years.

The image of the Edwardian period as a golden sunset of empire is an enduring and attractive one. Even today, when somebody talks of Edwardian Britain, it summons up for most of us images of grand garden parties and vintage motor cars driven by wealthy men, rather than soldiers gunning down strikers in the north of England. There is a reason for this attachment to the ludicrous idea that the years leading up to the First World War were part of a lost golden age. The whole idea of 'La Belle Epoque' did not appear before the 1920s. After the hideous slaughter which took place across Europe between 1914 and 1918, the long, hot summer of 1911 probably did feel like a golden age. The peace itself which had lasted in Europe since the end of the Franco-Prussian War over forty years before 1914, must have seemed like a dream. So much changed in the aftermath of the war, and not for the better, that it became quite common to blame the First World War for anything which was wrong with the world in the 1920s.

Edwardian Britain illustrates two of the mythic narratives beloved of the British and segues smoothly into a third. The golden age archetype is the dominant theme of this era, but events at that time were heavily bound up with the idea of foreigners swarming across the English Channel and occupying the country. This 'Invaders from the East' motif is as popular now as it was a century or so ago; as may be seen from current anxieties about immigration. The period ends with another well-known feature of British history, when the country had to send military forces across the channel to sort out Europe's difficulties. This is the subject of the next chapter.

Chapter 9

British Generals of the First World War 1914–1918: 'Lions led by Donkeys'

F ew of us know very much about the First World War, other than that it was fought about a hundred years ago, was an exceedingly bloody affair and involved Britain, France, Germany and America. There are half-remembered foreign place-names such as Gallipoli, Jutland and the Dardanelles and also a few names of famous people, Lloyd George, Kaiser Wilhelm and of course Field Marshal Haig. Beyond that, the details tend to be rather sketchy. One thing that everybody *does* know, though, is that the British generals of the First World War were criminally incompetent – callous butchers who wantonly sacrificed the lives of countless young soldiers in order to gain another few yards of muddy ground. How do we know this? It's hard to say, because few of us have troubled actually to read up on the military history of that war. It is just one of those things which are part of our heritage or shared cultural experience.

For the present generation, it is axiomatic that senior officers like Haig were upper-class types who viewed the men of their army as no more than cannon-fodder, pawns to be thrown into battle as part of a dreadful and pointless war of attrition. Wave upon wave of these hapless victims were ordered 'over the top' into No Man's Land, where they were mown down by German machine guns. So powerful is this image, that it is rarely questioned, being taken rather as a given in any conversation about the First World War. If ever we *do* take the trouble to ask ourselves about how we know all this, the conclusion reached is that it must be some kind of folk memory, which has presumably been passed down from father to son for a century or so. British soldiers advancing across No Man's Land towards the waiting, German machine guns, may be seen in Illustration 17. This then is the myth as we have received it. A small group of heartless generals and field marshals, all of them privately-educated, upper-class types, who took the flower of English youth and hurled them into conditions of unimaginable horror on the battlefields of France. Those who objected to sacrificing their lives in this purposeless way were executed by firing squads for their 'cowardice' or desertion. For most of us, this view of the British generals of the First World War is almost axiomatic: whatever else might be debated about the conflict, this particular aspect is taken for granted.

It might come as something of a surprise to readers to learn that our modern interpretation of what was known at the time as the 'Great War' does not represent the authentic views, by and large, of those who actually fought in it. When Field Marshal Douglas Haig, by that time an Earl, died in 1928, his funeral was the occasion of an outpouring of national grief comparable in scale and intensity to the mourning which followed Princess Diana's death in 1997. Hundreds of thousands of people, many of them former soldiers, lined the route of his funeral cortege. There would be nothing like it again until the funeral of Winston Churchill in 1965. Whoever else might criticize Haig, he was beloved by the men who had served under him. The name 'Douglas' became very popular in Britain during the 1920s as old soldiers named their sons after their former Commander-in-Chief. Seldom was a public figure so loved and respected by ordinary people. The idea of Haig as a heartless butcher certainly did not originate with the soldiers who had actually fought at the Battle of the Somme. Haig may be seen in Illustration 18.

Our present image of generals like Haig, as uncaring, Colonel Blimp types, does not date from the time of the First World War at all, but is rather a creation of the 1960s, a time when many of the old certainties were being thrown overboard and iconoclasm was all the rage. A well-known figure like Field Marshal Haig, still recalled fondly at the beginning of the 1960s by many men who had actually fought under him, was the perfect target for those who sought to blacken the names of anybody whom they saw as being part of 'the Establishment', either past or present. In 1960, the First World War had only been over for a little over forty years and so it was very much recent history. Of course, there had been criticism of Haig's tactics during battles such as the Somme before, most notably in Lloyd George's memoirs, published after Haig's death, but it was in the 1960s that the negative opinion of Haig and the other generals became the received wisdom, rather than just one point of view among many.

The quotation at the beginning of this chapter comes from the book which fired the opening shot in the campaign to create a new popular image for men like Haig and his colleagues General Sir Henry Wilson and Field Marshal Sir John French. In 1961, a young historian called Alan Clark published a book called *The Donkeys*, which portrayed Haig and his army colleagues as being cold-blooded and uncaring, wishing to win the war at whatever cost in human lives. The title was a reference to a supposed conversation between the German generals Ludendorff and Hoffmann during the war. Ludendorff was said to have remarked to Hoffmann that the English soldiers fought like lions, to which the other man replied, 'True. But don't we know that they are lions led by donkeys.' It is doubtful if this exchange ever really took place: Alan Clark was very cagy about his source for the quotation and it may be regarded as apocryphal. It is not in any case an original idea. Writing 2,000 years ago Plutarch observed that, 'An army of deer commanded by a lion is more to be feared than an army of lions led by a deer'.

There had been criticism before of Haig's conduct of the war and also the way in which his fellow generals seemed unable to adapt to the changing conditions of modern warfare; clinging to Victorian ideas, for instance the use of cavalry, rather than embracing new technology such as machine guns, aeroplanes and tanks. Clark's book *The Donkeys* and the thesis which it advanced might have passed unnoticed by the general public had it not been, improbably enough, turned into a musical, a rare event indeed for a non-fiction work of military history! Perhaps it is something of an exaggeration to say that *The Donkeys* became a musical, but not much: there is a good deal of truth in the idea.

A little over eighteen months after the publication of Clark's book, a new musical opened at the Theatre Royal in East London. Developed by Joan Littlewood, *Oh! What a Lovely War* featured many of the most famous music-hall songs from the First World War. This was no exercise in nostalgia, however. It was rather a savage denunciation of the British generals, including of course Haig. The soldiers in the production wore pierrot costumes, lending them a grotesque and ridiculous appearance. The portrayal of Haig was so offensive to some, that his family made strenuous efforts to stop the show being transferred to the West End, where it would of course be seen by far greater audiences than was the case in the little theatre in East London where it had opened. In 1969, *Oh! What a Lovely War* was turned into a major film, starring John Gielgud, Laurence Olivier, Vanessa Redgrave and Kenneth More. This cemented in the public mind the notion of Haig and the other generals as clown-like and out-of-touch figures who were responsible, because of their foolish and blinkered attitudes, for much of the carnage on the Western Front.

In the 1960s, it was recognized that books like *The Donkeys*, along with the film of *Oh! What a Lovely War,* really represented radical and revisionist views of the First World War. They were daring and ran counter to the generally-accepted interpretation of the war. By the 1970s though, this revisionist perspective on a major event in British history had somehow become, in the public mind at least, the orthodox version of history. Since then, this myth has been massively reinforced by another piece of popular culture; a satirical television comedy set during the period and starring Rowan Atkinson. Incredibly, episodes of this situation comedy are now widely used in secondary schools for teaching the history of the First World War!

In the autumn of 1989 the fourth and final series of the popular historical sitcom *Blackadder* was aired by the BBC. *Blackadder Goes Forth* was set in a trench on the Western Front during the First World War and showed how Captain Edmund Blackadder, played by Rowan Atkinson, attempted to survive the war by means of various stratagems. A key figure in the drama was Tony Robinson, playing Blackadder's hapless batman Private Baldrick. Baldrick is the archetypal 'everyman', a simple person caught up in events of which he has little understanding and over which he is able to exercise no control at all. On the face of it, his character and position are in sharp contrast to the well-educated officer whom he serves, but as the series progresses, it becomes apparent that both are merely pawns in the machinations of various senior officers, obvious fools, who have no regard at all for the lives of the troops under their command. Needless to say, General Haig makes an appearance.

Part of the appeal of *Blackadder Goes Forth* lies in the way that both Blackadder and Baldrick are shown to be little men, each struggling in their own way to overcome authority. They do this not by fighting openly against those above them, but rather by various 'cunning plans'. It was perhaps this appeal to the ancient mythic archetype of the little person using craftiness and subtlety against superiors, rather than open rebellion, which made the programme such a success. There are echoes here of Jaroslav Hasek's First World War classic, *The Good Soldier Svejk*.

Within a very few years, *Blackadder Goes Forth* was being treated not as an extravagant fantasy, but as a realistic parody of the actual situation of ordinary soldiers at the time that the comedy was set. True, it was wildly exaggerated and grotesque, but the actual premise upon which it was based, the thesis advanced by both Alan Clark and Joan Littlewood in the 1960s, was assumed by viewers to be historically accurate. This was a truly extraordinary situation, that a controversial minority perception of an important period of British history had been shaped by a musical and its film adaptation and was now treated universally as being the correct view of the past. A new offensive on the Western Front was described in *Blackadder* in these terms: 'Haig is about to make yet another gargantuan effort to move his drinks cabinet six inches closer to Berlin.'

The transformation of General Haig, as he was in 1916, from revered, national hero to blundering butcher was now complete. Episodes of the BBC comedy are regularly shown to school pupils studying history for GCSE and a new generation are thus indoctrinated with the myth of the British generals of that period. That Haig was at one time thought of by most people as one of the finest military figures of the age is quite unknown to almost everybody in Britain. A myth which has its origins barely fifty years ago has now become the standard version of history which is taught to the rising generation.

For many readers, it has probably come as something of a surprise that there *is* any other way of looking at the First World War generals; other, that is, than the one familiar to them from television and films. It is time now to look at what really happened in France a century ago and try to work out the extent to which Haig and the others were culpable and if so, to what extent. We shall also be asking ourselves why this myth took such rapid hold in people's minds decades after the end of the war. What was it about the *Blackadder* version of history which appeals so greatly to us that we prefer it to the historical facts? The influence of this mythic version of history is extremely strong and overshadows any modern war or even possibility of armed conflict. When we think of senior generals, at the back of our mind is the popular image of Haig, sacrificing all those young men so needlessly on the fields of France.

For almost the whole of human history prior to 1914, battlefields were places of movement and change. One side charged and the other either gave way or counter-attacked and charged in its turn. Cavalry was used to make breakthroughs and then infantry followed up and occupied the ground won in this way. This was the way that wars had always been fought, from Biblical times until Waterloo. Warfare was a mobile activity which entailed advances and retreats, attacks and counter-attacks. The movement around the battlefield was always about gaining an advantage. Sometimes, this could be achieved by sending forces round to one side and then striking your opponent in his unprotected flank. At others, a retreat might be feigned, in order to lure the enemy into a heedless rush which would end in an ambush by superior forces lying wait. Although there had been sieges in recent years where an attacker sat and tried to starve or bombard a fortress or town into submission, these were only minor episodes in wider campaigns which consisted, as in the past, of rapid, mobile conflict.

When the British army went to the aid of Belgium in 1914, there was no reason at all to think that this war was going to be different from any other and indeed to begin with, there was plenty of excitement as the British and French armies fought to hold back the Germans and prevent them from encircling Paris. It was when the battling armies ground to a halt that all the old ideas of warfare had to be abandoned and new tactics devised to cope with a wholly unexpected situation. that of static, rather than mobile battlefields.

During the early years of the twentieth century it became increasingly apparent that Germany and Britain would sooner or later be confronting each other. There were several false starts before the actual beginning of the war in 1914. The ostensible cause of Britain's declaration of war in the summer of that year was Germany's violation of Belgian neutrality, which had been guaranteed by Britain many years previously in the Treaty of London of 1839. When Germany went to war with France in the first days of August 1914, their plan of attack called for German troops to bypass the heavily-fortified frontier between France and Germany and instead to sweep through Belgium and into France, striking towards Paris from the north. It was an audacious plan, but it didn't quite come off.

There were several fast-moving military engagements in the opening weeks of the First World War; Mons, the Marne, the first Battle of Ypres. These were traditional battles, with the fortunes of the opposing sides changing rapidly. The British and Germans were both trying desperately to gain an advantage over each other, by moving their forces around the side and attacking the enemy from the flank. The forces moved back and forth and, for the first month or two at least, it really seemed that this was going to be a brisk and decisive war; one which would be over by Christmas. In the old days, it was true, wars dragged on for years, decades or even over a century, but with modern technological advances and with the resources of industrial societies behind them, it would not take too long before one country or another was able to deliver a knockout blow and bring matters to an end.

Such predictions of swift victory appeared to be borne out in September, when after making a rapid advance, the Germans began a general retreat. In their enthusiasm to encircle Paris, the Germans had left wide gaps between their forces, into which the British Expeditionary Force was able to drive. Realizing that their flanks were now exposed, the German commanders ordered a general retreat, back towards their own country. For five glorious days, the British drove the Germans back and there was talk among high-ranking Allied officers of the possibility of their being in Germany within a month. On 14 September, the exhausted German troops halted at the River Aisne. There, something quite unexpected happened.

Having stopped at the Aisne, the Germans chose to make a stand and fox-holes were dug, essentially, no more than holes in which men might shelter from enemy fire. Then machine guns were set up behind mounds of earth as a defensive measure. To everybody's amazement, the machine guns were able to turn back the whole force of Allied infantry. It was as simple as that. Men marching on foot were simply no match for automatic weapons. The Allies halted in turn and then, seeing that frontal assaults were impossible, tried to move to the side, in other words, find their way around the devas-tating machine-gun fire. They set up machine-gun posts of their own and of course the Germans then did their best to begin outflanking the Allies, so that they too could move forward.

As both armies were engaged in the same tactic, they moved towards the coast, each seeking that breakthrough moment when they would be able to strike at the flank and then encircle the enemy. This never actually happened and of course once the sea was reached, there were no more flanks to be attacked. At this point, and with the realization that frontal assaults were suicidal, the only option was to dig in and wait for some new development which would change things.

Both machine guns and barbed wire had been in use for years, but now they came into their own. Once it had been discovered that a few men hid-ing behind mounds of earth and operating machine guns could hold off a vastly superior force of enemy troops charging towards them, and both the Germans and British discovered this interesting and novel fact at about the same time, it led inevitably to both sides digging holes and hiding in them, while their machine guns protected them from potential attackers. This was at first regarded as a temporary expedient: nobody could possibly have known at that time that this stalemate would last for years.

In a sense, the British army were fighting on home territory in France and the southern part of Belgium. They had of course been here before and at one time, during the Angevin dynasty, this area had been British territory. The Battle of Agincourt had been fought here and Waterloo was just a little to the north. When Arthur Machen wrote his short story about the spec-tral bowmen of Agincourt who had aided the British Expeditionary Force at Mons (see Chapter 2), he was evoking this British familiarity with the muddy fields of this part of western Europe.

The dugouts in which troops sheltered gradually developed into a line of trenches which stretched from Switzerland to the English Channel. These were strictly defensive earthworks and anybody attacking them was likely to be mown down by machine-gun fire. In such a situation, there could be no movement and no battles in the conventional meaning of the word. This then was what became known as the 'Western Front', to distinguish it from the other theatres of war such as the Russian front to the east, and southern campaigns such as the fight for the Dardanelles and the landings at Gallipoli, in Turkey.

Things soon became very embarrassing for leaders and politicians on both sides of the trenches. The Kaiser had told troops that they would be home, 'before the leaves fell', because the German plans were predicated on France being defeated in six weeks or so. In Britain too, the expectation was for a short, sharp clash, which would end in a decisive victory for Britain and France. And now, as far as those in Britain and Germany could see, the soldiers were just sitting quietly and doing nothing at all. It was all most disappointing!

Of course, the officers commanding the troops on the Western Front knew what those at home did not, that an attack was the quickest and surest way to defeat. The Germans understood this very well, although it contradicted of course Clausewitz' most famous dictum that, 'The best defence is attack'. Besides, they were already winning, in a sense, because they had established themselves on French territory and only had to sit tight to look as though they had achieved at least some of their aims. The British and French, on the other hand, were left looking impotent and helpless. Here was the mightiest empire the world had ever known and they couldn't even advance their troops a few yards against an implacable foe.

For the British in particular, it appeared to be an insoluble conundrum. They were quite unable to shift the Germans from their positions inside France and nor did there appear to be any other weak spot, besides the Western Front, where it might be possible to strike at the Germans, in other words, a way to drive home an attack on their flank. The Balkans were tried, landings in Turkey were tried, action in the Middle East was attempted: none of it had the slightest effect upon the deadlocked battlefield of northern France. Not for nothing did those other theatres become known as 'sideshows'. When, after a protracted period of trench warfare, the British tried to force their way through the German lines by means of a frontal assault, it proved to be disastrous. In retrospect, it is easy to see why this should have been.

The lesson of Agincourt was, or should have been, that if footsoldiers attack across a field of mud towards an enemy who has a strong, defensive position and is able to project death over a distance of half a mile or more, then the attackers are likely to come off worse by a considerable margin.

This was certainly how it had been at Agincourt. Hindsight is a wonderful thing and it is upon this that all criticism of the British generals of the First World War is based. How could they not see that they were about to replay Agincourt; only this time, being on the losing side of the battle? The answer is of course that there had been so many exciting innovations in warfare over the half millennium since Agincourt, that the picture appeared to people like Haig to have changed utterly. Aeroplanes! Telephones! Heavy artillery! Railways! Radio! Barbed wire! Machine guns! Petrol engines! How could one possibly compare military activity in the twentieth century with that at the time of the Hundred Years War?

It is possible to have some sympathy with this perspective; however it might have proved in the long run to have been hopelessly wrong. Of course, all the new technology must have looked like a game-changer to the senior officers a century ago. The flaw in their thinking only gradually came to light and it was bitter experience which taught them, and us, how mistaken they were in their evaluation of the military position on the Western Front in 1915 and 1916. Their error was simple, but devastating. The technological advances which appeared to alter the nature of warfare so radically, all related to defence: they gave a very strong advantage to defenders, but none at all to the attacker. It was this which doomed the efforts of men like Generals French and Haig when they were planning their 'big push', the one which would bring about the much longed for 'breakthrough'.

Take aeroplanes, for example. These were a great novelty, which had only been around for a little over ten years when the First World War began. Exciting as they might have seemed, their role was limited to begin with to reconnaissance. They were no use for supporting ground forces in an attack. Railways were very useful for bringing reinforcements to the front to defend against an enemy attack, but they too were useless as a tool of offensive war. Machine guns and barbed wire were primarily defensive weapons and even artillery was often of more use to an enemy than it was to the attacking side. Its use gave early warning that an assault was about to be mounted. Petrol-driven road vehicles were, like railway trains, very good for bringing troops to the front, but not the least help during an attack.

One can hardly blame those designing strategies at the time for breaking the stalemate of trench warfare for not being prescient enough to see all this, when it was only years after the event that military historians were able to analyse the course of the war and work out just how things had gone so badly wrong. One thing was certain and that was that a defensive strategy could not be pursued indefinitely by the British. In effect, such a course of action would mean that the Germans had won the war, by continuing to occupy Belgium, the invasion of which had of course been the original *casus belli*. If the deadlock was not broken, it might lead too to a negotiated compromise settlement with Germany, which would also be a political disaster for the British government. With many British soldiers dead and the huge popular support for the war, making any kind of concessions to Germany would be an act of suicide on the part of any politician at Westminster.

It was for failing to get things moving on the Western Front that the commander-in-chief of the BEF, Sir John French, was sacked at the end of 1915. The new C-in-C, Douglas Haig, knew that he would have to take decisive action if he wished to retain his post. That is not to say that he was prepared to throw men's lives away with gay abandon, in the way that he is popularly portrayed as doing, more that Haig was determined to come up with schemes which would, by breaking through the German lines in northern France, bring the war to an end.

This then was the bind into which the senior officers of the British army found themselves after eighteen months of trench warfare in France. Various means of breaking the deadlock other than by a direct frontal assault on the German lines had been tried. The attempt to supply Russia via the Mediterranean, by opening up the Dardanelles had proved a failure and in the early summer of 1916 came a great naval encounter in the North Sea, the Battle of Jutland. This was inconclusive and left matters in France just as they had been before.

The Germans were now mounting an offensive of their own, on the French fortress of Verdun, and it was partly to relieve pressure on this key position that Haig and the other generals agreed to launch what was intended to be a decisive stroke against Germany at the Somme. It is this battle which has come, in the minds of many, to typify the needless slaughter of the Western Front during the First World War. This is a little strange, because for forty or fifty years after the end of the war, it was Passchendaele, otherwise known as the Third Battle of Ypres, which was, until the 1960s, known as a byword for the brutality and waste of those years. The adoption of the Somme as a new symbol dates only from that time.

It is customary to describe the Battle of the Somme as opening on 1 July 1916, when wave after wave of British infantry went 'over the top' and marched towards the waiting German machine guns. In fact, it was a week earlier, on 24 June, that the fighting really began. The greatest artillery barrage the world had ever known began on that day and continued for an entire week, pounding away remorselessly at the German trenches and the No

Man's Land which lay in front of them. The aim was both to cut the barbed wire entanglements which, in the usual way of things, prevented British soldiers from advancing across No Man's Land, and also of course to pulverise the German dugouts and trenches. As General Sir Henry Rawlinson, who directed most of the operation in the field, said, 'Nothing could exist at the conclusion of the bombardment in the area covered by it.' The reality was rather different.

The attack on the Somme was launched along a 25-mile long sector and it was the whole of this which had been subjected to that ferocious artillery attack. Because of the sheer size of the area being shelled and because the attack had been in depth, covering No Man's Land as well as the trenches themselves, the fire of the British guns had been greatly diluted. This was a random, blanket barrage, rather than surgical strikes against particular targets. Many of the shells which were fired were defective, falling into the mud and causing no more harm than a watery splash. Even worse, the effect of explosives upon coils of barbed wire was not really known at that time. The hope was that the shells would shred the wire into tiny fragments, leaving the way clear for the advancing infantry. In fact, much of the barbed wire was simply thrown up into the air by the force of the explosions, falling back to earth even more tangled and impassable than before!

Perhaps the greatest miscalculation was the killing rate of the shells fired at the German positions. For all that Rawlinson believed that nothing could remain alive after the week-long attack, just 2,500 German soldiers had been killed. The remainder, guessing that when the artillery fell silent the infantry assault would begin, simply climbed out of their dugouts and began training their machine guns at the soldiers picking their way through No Man's Land. Twenty thousand British soldiers were killed on that first day of infantry action on the Somme, the greatest slaughter ever endured by the British army in a single day.

The next day, the assault was renewed and the fighting on this front continued until November. In the south of the area, the Germans were driven back a few miles, but there was no decisive breakthrough, such as would allow the war to become mobile once more. All that happened was that the German trench systems were reformed seven miles rear of the old ones and there they remained for another two years, despite the best efforts of the British and French.

Since it is upon actions like those on the Somme that most of the criticism of the British generals are based, we must ask what, if anything, the fighting there actually achieved in the long run; in other words, if the terrible death toll did anything at all to bring the war any closer to an end. The answer is, perhaps surprisingly to modern audiences, that the Somme was a turning point in the First World War and although it may be seen in the short term as a tactical failure, it was of crucial strategic importance in defeating Germany and ending the war. In short, it was a great strategic victory, masterminded by Haig.

Until the summer of 1916, it had been possible for the German high command to regard the British army with a certain amount of contempt. They were, after all, not a professional army, but largely a volunteer force, a rag-tag assortment of clerks, bricklayers, shop assistants and factory workers. How could such men hope to stand up to the Prussian military tradition which embodied the Kaiser's armed forces? The answer was, after the Somme, that they could not only face up to the German army, but could more than hold their own on the battlefield against them. One German staff officer offered this comment after the fighting had ended, 'The Somme was the muddy grave of the German field army.' For Germany, at least, there was no doubt that this was a British victory, even though the Germans managed to cling on to the territory that they had seized two years earlier. It was plain after the Somme that Britain, with its mighty industrial capacity and the backing of the greatest empire the world had ever known, was more than a match for German ambitions.

This gloomy acceptance that victory against Britain was unlikely to be achieved by force of arms alone, prompted the Germans to embark upon a strategy which practically guaranteed their defeat, although they did not of course realize this at the time. Since the Somme showed them that the best they could do was hang on against the British forces, it was decided to attempt an indirect attack upon the British nation. This was to be done by isolating the country from the rest of the world and preventing any imports of food or other supplies. After their bruising encounter at Jutland, the German High Seas Fleet did not leave harbour again for the whole of the war. This meant that if Britain was to be blockaded and ultimately starved into submission, then submarines would be the weapon to use. After all, the British were themselves operating a very effective naval blockade of Germany, refusing to allow any supplies to enter the country by sea. This was causing hardship in Germany and it was thought that an even more severe blockade of Britain might swiftly bring the country to its knees and force the British to sue for peace.

The German leaders believed that a policy of unrestricted submarine warfare might bring Britain to critical shortages of food and other necessities of life within just six months, which would the British to sue for peace.

For this to be effective, the German submarines would have to sink any ship, of any nationality, found in British waters. Since many American ships plied the route across the Atlantic, it was inevitable that this strategy would eventually draw America into the war, but in Germany, it was hoped that Britain would be finished before this happened. It was a fatal miscalculation. Forty-eight hours after Germany began to conduct unrestricted submarine warfare, America broke off diplomatic relations with Germany. Two months later, America declared war on Germany, a direct consequence of the activities of the U-boats, which was in turn a result of the fighting on the Somme. With America fighting alongside Britain, the result of the war could be in no doubt. The Somme had, in effect, brought about victory over Germany.

It is certainly true that many soldiers were killed on the Western Front during the First World War, but the idea that men like Haig were squandering lives needlessly is a foolish one, however much it has over the past half century become the received orthodoxy. Haig was given the job of beating Germany and he did his best to accomplish this end. If any criticism is to made, then it should perhaps be directed more at his political masters than the soldier charged with devising schemes to beat Germany on the battlefield.

In the years following the end of the First World War, Haig was enormously popular with ordinary people, not least the men who had actually served on the Western Front and even taken part in the Battle of the Somme. The distorted version of this military leader with which we are all familiar today has its roots in the writing of those who were not even born until after the First World War had ended.

The British generals of 1914 to 1918 did the best that they could with what they had available to them in manpower and resources, and ultimately they won the war for Britain. By the 1960s, the patriotism shown by ordinary men who volunteered for the army was seen as an embarrassing anachronism and was an easy target for a more cynical age. So vivid were the images with which these writers of both fiction and non-fiction juggled, that they have stuck in our minds in a way that mere facts and figures can never do. That the whole war was a variation of the old story of Britain going to Europe to sort out their mess, made those years ready for mythologizing of this sort.

The First World War is recalled today with shock at the way in which those in high office conducted themselves in relation to the ordinary rank and file. The Second World War, on the other hand, is still thought of with pride as representing the best of the British spirit in action. It is that conflict at which we shall be looking in the final chapter.

Chapter 10

The Battle of Britain 1940:
'So much, owed by so many, to so few'

We come now to the apotheosis of British myth-making, a sequence of events covering a year or so which combines almost all the mythic themes at which we have been looking. Britain with its back to the wall; Britain as champion of democracy and the rule of law; Britain as island nation; Britain under threat from invaders from the East; Britain as the country which sorts out Europe's mess; Britain as the home of sangfroid and stiff upper lips; Britain as David, in the David and Goliath mythic narrative. There was even, before the year had ended, a deliberate, self-conscious and highly successful attempt to shape 1940 into part of a 'golden age' story, a time at which those alive then, would look back upon in later years with satisfaction and nostalgia. In a sense, the period which we will examine in this chapter pulls together all the individual threads at which we have looked and weaves them all into one glorious tapestry.

The Battle of Britain and the Blitz which swiftly followed it in 1940 have been the subject of so much commentary and interpretation that it might be thought that there is little new or original to say on the subject. The idea of those events during the Second World War as exemplifying Britain's own particular mythos has, however, seldom been explored.

It is intriguing to analyse ancient myths, such as that of the Biblical great flood, and try to untangle fact from fiction. Fascinating as this exercise is, it is ultimately unsatisfying, because we are never likely to be able to settle the matter once and for all. By definition, there are no written records of prehistoric lives and so we are compelled to piece things together from the archaeological evidence. Tracing the development of myths in historical times is quite a different matter, because we often have many eyewitness accounts and also a wealth of physical remains to examine. From the beginning of the twentieth century, we also have photographs, films and sound recordings to assist our investigations. From the middle of that century, there are still living eyewitnesses who may be questioned. This means that often the facts are not really in dispute at all. It is how those facts are viewed and the interpretation put upon them by succeeding generations which allows us to chart the growth of the myth surrounding the historical events. Nowhere is this more true than when looking at how people today think about the experience of the Second World War, as it was for those who lived in Britain during the opening years of the conflict.

As in previous chapters, we shall start by looking at the myth as it is widely accepted and then see what this might tell us about those who created it. We shall also look at bits of the historical record which have been altered or altogether omitted in order to enhance the mythic narrative and make it more impressive. A lot of this has happened in the case of the Battle of Britain, which was fought in the skies above this country, and also in connection with the aerial bombardment of Britain's cities which became known as the 'Blitz'.

In 1940, the year following Britain's declaration of war against Germany, the country stood alone. Poland and France had fallen, the British army had retreated from the Continent in the course of the disastrous rout which became known as the Dunkirk Evacuation and it seemed only a matter of time before the Germans crossed the Channel and invaded Britain. At that crucial juncture in British history, the country stood alone, single-handedly defying the might of Nazi Germany. As Churchill put it, future generations would say, 'This was their finest hour'. When the German air force tried to seize control of the air above and around the British Isles, a tiny handful of brave pilots fought them off, until the Nazis resorted to the cowardly tactic of deliberately targeting civilians by bombing the larger cities. Even then, Britain showed that she could 'take it'. Vastly outnumbered and ill-equipped, with no allies, the country soldiered on until an alliance was forged which eventually resulted in the defeat of the Nazi dictatorship and the triumph of democracy over fascism.

Even at the time that this beautiful and heroic mythic narrative was being constructed, there were those who recognized how preposterous it was, but at the same time realized that the myth was in many ways more important than the bare facts. The French author and critic Georges Bernanos was living in exile in South America at the time of the Battle of Britain. He wrote that the story as it was being told then was, 'a fairy-tale, a tale that no serious adult, no man of ability or experience, could possibly understand – a children's tale'. It is in this sense that we must look at the accepted story of the Battle of Britain and try to understand why it proved so useful to the people living in the country at that time.

One of the reasons that so many nations, religions and cultures have developed a mythos is that is that such a body of myths about their history and character gives individual people an idea about themselves with which they can identify, and serves to make them feel that they are part of something bigger and more important than themselves. This feeling can become a self-fulfilling prophecy and help actually to strengthen a national or religious identity or even create one where none previously existed. One thinks, for example, of the Nazis' conscious appeal to the pagan myths of the early Germanic peoples and how useful this was in creating a mighty nation from the miserable, defeated country which was scraping an existence in the aftermath of the Versailles Peace Treaty during the 1920s. What Georges Bernanos called a 'fairy-tale' was a grand synthesis of all the myths which the British had acquired over the centuries; a wonderful mixture of truth, legend, exaggeration and downright falsehood which worked a special magic and changed the course of history.

Before untangling the myth, we must first understand the background which led to the aerial campaign known as the Battle of Britain. The facts are simple enough and relatively uncontroversial. Throughout the 1930s, the ruler of Germany, Adolf Hitler, had been pursuing an expansionist policy in Europe, which was designed to swallow up neighbouring countries and allow Germany to dominate the continent. Once Austria and half of Czechoslovakia had been absorbed by Germany in this way, Hitler's eyes turned east, towards Poland. Before the First World War, much of what was in 1939 called Poland had been an integral part of Germany and the aim was to take back what was seen by many Germans as their own land. Britain and France, however, had promised to defend Poland against any aggression and when Germany attacked and invaded Poland on 1 September 1939, both countries declared war on Germany. The Second World War had begun.

There followed the period known as the 'Phoney War', when, despite a state of war supposedly existing between Britain and Germany, nothing much seemed to happen. This came to an abrupt end in April 1940, with the German invasion of Denmark and Norway. The following month, Holland and Belgium were also invaded and an attack launched on France. The British Army went to the aid of France and was defeated, forced into an ignominious retreat from the coastal town of Dunkirk. From France's signing of an armistice with Germany on 22 June 1940 until the German invasion of Russia, exactly a year later on 22 June 1941, it is traditional to assert that Britain 'stood alone' against the might of Nazi Germany, which now ruled most of Europe. Winston Churchill, in his speeches, relied heavily on this theme, emphasizing that those in the island of Britain were alone against the greatest power of the age.

On 18 June 1940, four days before the French signed the armistice, Winston Churchill gave a famous speech in which he explicitly stated that the people in Britain were standing alone and that they were all that stood between Hitler and world domination. This speech, in which the phrase, 'this was their finest hour' was used, consciously calls upon the various myths which would resonate with the people in Britain, emphasizing their special status and unique importance in world affairs. There is the image of Britain as the nation which will sort out Europe's problems for it and stand up for fair play; 'we abate nothing of our just demands – Czechs, Poles, Norwegians, Dutch, Belgians, all who have joined their causes to our own shall be restored'. There is the claim that Britain is the only nation which can save 'Christian civilization' and, by implication, democracy and the rule of law; 'the Battle of Britain is about to begin. Upon this battle depends the survival of Christian civilization. Upon it depends our own British life . . .'. An appeal is made to the notion of Britain as an island nation and it is suggested that everything depends solely upon the people living in Britain: 'Hitler knows he will have to break us in this island or lose the war.' Underlying it all, the theme if you like, is that old familiar idea that Britain fights best when its back is against the wall. And there is too the 'Invaders from the East' motif at which we have looked when examining the Spanish Armada and Battle of Waterloo. Finally, we observe that Churchill, even before what he was calling already the Battle of Britain had begun, was telling people that this was to be a wonderful time in British history and that a thousand years later it would be regarded as Britain's 'finest hour'. The idea that those alive at that time in Britain were living through a 'golden age' of heroism and chivalry was being deliberately and consciously evoked.

Of course, much of this speech was, for all the grand language, mere cant. Churchill himself was paying only lip service to the high ideals expressed in it. It was all well and good for him to talk about the 'just demands' on behalf of the Czechs, Norwegians, Poles, Belgians and Dutch, but in his private capacity he showed only contempt for these nations, as he demonstrated when dining at the Savoy in 1940. The BBC at that time ended their Sunday programmes by playing the national anthems of all those nations whose causes Britain was supporting, often by sheltering their royal families and various other refugees. Churchill called a waiter over after the first three anthems had been played and said, 'Pray turn off that wireless. Enough of that Beggar's Opera!'

The thesis outlined in the speech above, which was delivered to the House of Commons and is perhaps Churchill's most famous, is plain: everything hinges upon the British people, that is to say those actually living in the island of Britain. The island nation stands alone. This particular aspect of the myth of the Battle of Britain may be fairly easily dispelled. Almost a quarter of the Earth's land surface was at that time part of the British Empire. Germany, by comparison, had only a handful of European territories at its disposal. With Canada, Australia, New Zealand, India, South Africa and various other countries and dependencies across Africa, Asia, South America and the Pacific on her side, it was perhaps stretching things a little to see Britain as the underdog in a confrontation with Germany! America too, although theoretically pursuing an isolationist policy, was in reality ready and willing to back Britain.

Leaving aside the empire upon which Britain would be able to call in the long term, what of the prospects for what Winston Churchill was already calling the Battle of Britain? How fair was the David and Goliath image to which Churchill was appealing: in other words, to what extent was Britain the underdog in the coming fight against Germany? Almost incredibly, the propaganda version of events has found its way into the history books and is still the standard version to which most people in Britain adhere almost eighty years later. That there is hardly any truth in this story has not prevented it from enduring to this day. A detailed examination of the individual elements of the story as it has come down to us might serve to make this a little clearer. We begin with a fairly minor example of the misconceptions held about this part of the Second World War.

It is popularly supposed that in the Battle of Britain, a small group of British RAF officers, most of them public-school types, engaged in dogfights over the skies of southern England, against a much greater force of German aircraft who were trying to establish air superiority above the English Channel. The German aim was to defeat the RAF and so pave the way for invasion of Britain. This, in a nutshell, is the first part of the mythical narrative at which we shall be looking; one which is still, for many, the accepted version of that period in 1940, a handful of gallant RAF officers, perhaps with handlebar moustaches, saving Britain from the Nazis.

Because this is a quintessentially British myth, it is only natural that in our imagination, the RAF pilots in 1940 should be British officers. Some were, but roughly half were not. Looking first at the notion that the pilots were British, we find to our surprise that of the RAF pilots who fought in the Battle of Britain, between July and October 1940, about a fifth were not born in this country. The RAF's roll of honour lists 2,350 British pilots during that period, along with 574 who were not British. These include over 140 Poles and eighty-five or so Czechs, along with Belgians, French, Australians and various other nationalities. These men boosted the numbers of pilots at that crucial time and helped win Britain's first major battle of the Second World War.

This enduring idea that the Battle of Britain was an exclusively British affair from this country's point of view has led to some grotesque situations. In 2009, for instance, during elections for the European Parliament, the British National Party decided to appropriate this myth for their own purposes. They used the image of a Spitfire from that period, above which was the slogan 'Battle for Britain'. This may be seen in Illustration 19. The poster was meant to evoke both the spirit of the Second World War and was also a reference to the 'Invaders from the East' element of British mythology, in this case, Eastern Europeans, who were supposedly flooding into the country with disastrous consequences for the native inhabitants. Perhaps because history was not their strong point, the propagandists of the BNP chose a photograph of a Spitfire belonging to a Polish squadron of the Royal Air Force. The complaints about Polish builders looked a little ungracious when we recall that Polish fighter pilots had been defending Britain from invasion in 1940.

The contribution of foreign-born pilots to the defence of Britain was no nominal or symbolic one. During the Battle of Britain, only two men managed to notch up a total of sixteen 'kills'. One of these men was English and the other a Czech called Josef František. Among those who were pilots during the Battle of Britain, the one who went on to gain the highest number of kills during the rest of the war was a South Africa called Adolph 'Sailor' Malan, who brought down thirty-two German planes in total. Without men such as these, the outlook for the RAF would have been somewhat bleaker.

As for all those RAF officers flying the fighters during the Battle of Britain, a third of them were nothing of the sort. They were sergeants or flight sergeants. The idea of working-class fighter pilots is a strange one to us, but it is certainly the case that when we take away the foreigners and NCOs, we find that only about half the pilots at that time were really British officers, some of whom were the product of public schools, although many were not.

Having dealt with a fairly minor distortion which has become part of the myth surrounding the Battle of Britain, it is time to consider how unequally matched the two sides were. For this is the crux of the matter, that the gallant 'few' were, and still are, represented as being vastly outnumbered in the air by the planes of the Luftwaffe. One side in this famous battle certainly had a notable advantage over the other, both technologically and from the point of view of material resources. The only thing is, it was not the Germans who had this strong advantage, but rather the British. All things taken into account, it would have been slightly surprising had Britain not won the contest against the German air force in the summer of 1940.

Transporting an invasion force across the Channel would have entailed the use of slow-moving barges or landing craft, very vulnerable to attack from the air or from ships of the Royal Navy stationed on the South Coast. To carry out this enterprise, the Germans needed to put the RAF out of action, so that they ruled the sky between France and Britain. This would enable them to use their own planes to attack any British naval vessels which threatened their seaborne invasion force. Rendering the Royal Air Force helpless would mean attacking the airfields of Kent, and nearby counties, with bombers. These bombers would be vulnerable to attack by British fighters and so an escort of their own fighters would be necessary to protect the bombers.

Fortunately, Britain had, during the 1930s, been following that famous Roman dictum, *Si vis pacem, para bellum*: 'If you want peace, then prepare for war'. At the very height of Neville Chamberlain's appeasement, a line of radar towers were being constructed along the East and South Coast of Britain to provide early warning of the arrival of German bombers. This network, called Chain Home, was very effective, allowing British operators to detect and give advance warning of the approach of German aeroplanes as soon as they took off from airfields in France. Little wonder then that these installations were among the first targets of the German bombing raids in 1940. Of course, nobody talked about 'radar' at the time. This was an Americanism which did not appear until 1943. The British referred to Radio Direction Finding or RDF for short.

The towers of Chain Home were built of girders and looked like enormous electricity pylons; one remaining one at Bawdsley is 365 feet tall. One of the towers may be seen in Illustration 20. In the last chapter, we saw that high explosives did not cut the barbed wire at the Battle of the Somme as the British had hoped. The blast simply passed through the rolls of wire, at best hurling them into the air and tangling them up. Much the same thing happened when the Germans bombed the radar stations in 1940. The nearby buildings were badly damaged, but the towers themselves were left unscathed. Most of the bomb damage was repaired in a matter of hours and only at the installation at Ventnor, on the Isle of Wight, was a base wrecked. Even then, it took only a matter of weeks to get this part of the system back into action. When the Germans found that attacking Chain Home was more difficult than they had expected, and not realizing how effective the British radar was, the efforts of the Luftwaffe were redirected against airfields.

This was the first major blunder of the campaign. Throughout the Battle of Britain, the RAF would always know ahead of time where the Germans were heading, so that they could be ready to intercept them.

The Chain Home towers and surrounding buildings were bombed on 9 August and then again on 11 and 12 August. The following day, with the radar system still largely intact and operational, the Luftwaffe launched '*Adlerangriff*', 'Eagle Day'. Waves of bombers, accompanied by fighters to protect them, began attacking the airfields of southern England. In all that day, around 1,500 German aeroplanes crossed the English Channel. The RAF lost thirteen fighters, compared to the forty-five planes of the Luftwaffe which were brought down. The all-out attack from the air continued the following day, 14 August, when 500 German planes flew across the Channel. This time, seventy of them were shot down, while the RAF lost only twenty-seven aircraft. It was clear by then that this was to be a war of attrition and the Germans hoped that they would be able to withstand their losses better than the British were able to bear their own.

One of the factors which had to be borne in mind by the Luftwaffe was that when they lost an aeroplane to enemy action, they almost invariably lost the crew as well as the machine itself. The RAF were fighting over Britain or the Channel. When a plane was hit, the pilot could bale out and parachute to safety. Sometimes, it was possible to crash-land and again, the pilot would live to fight another day, as indeed might the aircraft.

Certainly some RAF pilots were killed when their planes were brought down, but many were not. For the Germans, the case was entirely different. If a plane was brought down over Britain, then the crew, if they survived, were sure to be captured. Of the seventy planes which the Germans lost on 14 August, every single crew member was either killed or taken prisoner. By way of contrast, an RAF pilot who had parachuted to safety was sometimes able to hitch a lift back to his airfield and be back in the air that very day. For example, during an attack on Biggin Hill airfield on 30 August, seventeen German planes were shot down and only one British one. The pilot of that plane parachuted to safety, hitched a lift back to his base and was in action again before the end of the day! Sometimes, foreign pilots serving in the RAF had a rough time of it, because after parachuting from their stricken planes, they were mistaken for Germans and one or two were nearly lynched by angry civilians.

Another advantage that the RAF enjoyed in the Battle of Britain as a result of fighting on home territory was that their planes were able to land to refuel and take on fresh ammunition, a luxury denied to the Luftwaffe. After flying from France and crossing the English Channel, the German fighters had a mere twenty minutes of flying time over England. Those which went as far as London had even less. For them, there was just ten minutes above the British capital before they had to return to France to refuel. This meant that the German fighter pilots had to keep one eye on the clock for the whole time that they were fighting above England. If they did not disengage and run for home after a few minutes, they ran the risk of having to ditch their planes in the sea, as they ran out of fuel.

Sometimes, discussion about the Battle of Britain becomes bogged down in dissecting the rival merits of the different fighters and bombers deployed by one side or the other. The rate of climb of the German Messerschmitt Me 109Es, as opposed to the speed of the 110s, Spitfire versus Hurricane – that kind of thing. In an equal competition, matters such as speed and firepower would indeed be the deciding factors in a dogfight. However, when one of the contestants knows that he is in a desperate hurry and must break off the engagement after a few minutes, matters are not equal. The pilot who is able to nip down to earth and pick up more ammunition and fuel has a very distinct advantage. In this particular case, that strong edge was in the RAF's favour.

This war of attrition would be won when one side or the other ran out of aeroplanes or pilots to fly them. Despite the idea, sedulously peddled at that time, that the little island of Britain was struggling to cope with the onslaught of the military juggernaut which was Nazi Germany, the reality was somewhat different. Obviously, the aeroplanes being shot down were only one part of the picture – the German bombing raids were also destroying planes on the ground at the airfields which they hit. On 16 August, for instance, sixty aircraft were blown up at RAF Brize Norton and elsewhere. With Britain and Germany losing aeroplanes at the rate of dozens a day, the crucial factor would be which side was able more quickly to make up the deficiencies produced by the ferocious combat. The answer to this question was easy and we need only look at the production figures for aircraft over the summer and autumn of 1940 to see who was doing best at this aspect of the war:

	Britain	Germany
June	446	164
July	496	220
August	476	173
September	467	218
October	469	144

There can be little doubt who was winning the battle for production when we look at these statistics. One can also see at a glance one reason that Germany brought the Battle of Britain to a close, realizing that they were unlikely to be able to beat their enemy into submission by means of air power alone. By September, Germany was losing more planes than they were able to manufacture. Had they continued their military strategy against Britain, then the Luftwaffe would slowly have dwindled away.

The problem for Germany was that Hitler was already at this time planning the invasion of Russia and this would need armoured vehicles, in addition to aircraft. Because the Stuka dive-bomber had proved so effective against ground troops and armour, production of this had been maintained at the expense of heavier bombers and fighters. When used against British targets as part of a strategic bombing campaign the Stuka proved a disaster. The faster British fighters soon dealt with the slow-moving Stukas and they were withdrawn from operations over Britain. Factories in Germany, because so many and varied demands were being placed upon them, began to neglect some types of military hardware in favour of others. With Operation Barbarossa, the plan for the invasion of the Soviet Union, gearing up, production of tanks took precedence over aircraft. Incredible as it may seem, at the height of this phase of the war, between September 1940 and February 1941, production of aircraft in Germany actually fell by 40 per cent.

The Battle of Britain is traditionally seen as a desperate, defensive fight against an aerial assault which came after the end of the 'Phoney War'. There was fighting in Norway, France and the Low Countries and the British Expeditionary Force was evacuated from Dunkirk at the end of May and beginning of June. Then, there was a lull of a few months, before Germany launched air raids against Britain. The RAF fought back gamely and then, after the Germans began a more general bombing campaign, including cities, Britain hit back and began bombing Germany in retaliation. This too is part of the fairy tale. It is time to reveal that a little sleight of hand has been played upon the reader and certain crucial facts withheld relating to the Battle of Britain!

There are two reasons why the story of the Germans bombing Britain first during the Second World War is an important part of the myth of the Battle of Britain and the Blitz. The first reason is that this provided some justification for the horrors of the fire-bombing of Hamburg and Dresden later in the war. These dreadful attacks could to some extent be excused by pointing out that it was Germany who had first started bombing civilian targets and that they were therefore only reaping what they had sown.

The morality of this argument is, to say the least of it, open to question, but it at least provided a salve to the conscience of those worrying about the suffering which the RAF was inflicting upon innocent women and children. This is why, even today, one will hear people defend the bombing of German cities by saying that it was they who began this kind of attack and we were only repaying the Germans in the same coin.

The second motive for pretending that the Germans bombed Britain first is that this ties in more neatly with the struggling little country fighting back heroically against overwhelming odds image, upon which the whole mythic narrative depends. The story of the outnumbered RAF battling to fight back the waves of Luftwaffe bombers is moving only because the British air force was hopelessly outnumbered and fighting for the very survival of their country. Knowing that for months before the Battle of Britain had even begun, the RAF had been relentlessly pounding German cities with groups of a hundred or more bombers at a time, would make a nonsense of this 'Gallant Little Island' scenario; which is why we have done our best to bury this inconvenient truth by eradicating it from the national consciousness.

On the night of 11 May 1940, four months before the start of the Blitz, thirty-six British bombers attacked the German town of München-Gladbach. A great deal of damage was done to the centre of the town, although only four people were actually killed in the raid. Four days after the air raid on München-Gladbach, a hundred British bombers struck at the heart of Germany's industrial might, in the Ruhr. They primarily targeted oil tanks. Night after night, the bombing raids continued against railways and oil storage facilities across Germany. Of course, what we in Britain chiefly recall about May and June 1940 is not the bombing of German cities, but rather the evacuation from Dunkirk and the feeling that this country had its back to the wall and was barely able to survive against the Nazi peril. That every night for months, British bombers were flying across the North Sea and dropping hundreds of tons of bombs on Germany spoils the satisfying and neat sequence of events which has become an integral part of the British mythos. The British bombing of German cities, four months before the German air force bombed cities in Britain, was no half-hearted or symbolic affair. On 17 May, for instance, 130 bombers struck oil refineries and railway yards. In Hamburg, thirty-four people were killed when bombs struck the centre of the city.

Very few people in Britain today are aware that long before the Battle of Britain and the Blitz, the RAF was carrying out daily air raids on Germany, for months at a time. It jars a little, when we have for decades been asked to believe that Britain's air force was stretched to the very limit in the defence of the country, to learn that there were at that time hundreds of bombers in the air every day, inflicting great damage on cities such as Berlin and Hamburg.

Is it true though that Britain was standing alone at that time, never mind how powerful her air force might or might not have been? Unfortunately, this too is a fantasy. The Battle of Britain began in earnest on 9 August 1940. A few days later, on 14 August, the American President Franklin Roosevelt announced that he was giving Britain fifty warships, in exchange for American use of British bases in the Caribbean and the Atlantic. Two months later, a secret Anglo-American agreement was signed. Half of all the armaments and munitions produced in the United States would from then on be sent to Britain. Another 370 ships would be made available for Britain as well. For a country standing alone, Britain was doing pretty well.

In November 1940, the RAF made large-scale bombing raids deep into the heart of Germany. On 8 November, Hitler was due to give a speech in Munich to mark the anniversary of the so-called Beer Hall Putsch. His plans were disrupted by an air raid. That same night, 163 bombers struck Berlin and the following night over a hundred planes bombed Hamburg. The British bombing of Germany began months before the Blitz and continue unabated throughout it, for a total of five years. It was not Germany which began bombing British cities, but the other way round.

The myth of the Battle of Britain and the Blitz sum up and encapsulate all the myths at which we have been looking in this book. The overarching mythic theme of 1940 for Britain is the little man standing up against overwhelming forces, which describes both the average British citizen in the Blitz and also Britain as a country against the might of the Third Reich. The notion of the golden age was being fashioned by Churchill even before the Battle of Britain, when he talked of people in a thousand years saying of 1940s Britain that, 'this was their finest hour.' The familiar idea of Britain having to pop over to Europe and sort things out is also to be found, as too is the image of Britain as the bringer of justice and the rule of law. The whole edifice of archetypes is completed by the 'Invaders from the East', about to sweep across the English Channel and take over the country. Little wonder that whatever other stories of their past the British are happy to jettison, the days of the Blitz still retain the power to move and inspire.

Endword

We have in this book looked at ten historical episodes which illustrate neatly the mythic themes so beloved of the British nation. The underlying ideas which are associated with the stories in this book are more than mere historical or academic curiosities. They are still going strong and are now embraced as enthusiastically as ever they were at the height of the British Empire in the Victorian period. They have lost none of their appeal. One does not need to think hard in order to see where these archetypal myths are still flourishing today. The idea of the British 'golden age', for example, has moved with the times and is now no longer considered to be the age of the Edwardians or the time 'before the war'. Instead, it is thought by many to be the 1960s or 1970s, when the baby boomers were growing up. This was of course an enchanted and peaceful time, when little children could roam the streets safely all day without coming to any harm, as long as they were careful to return home by teatime. The other myths are similarly with us in new forms.

Britain as home of democracy and the rule of law is perhaps the most popular and enduring theme and is officially taught now to children, under the auspices of the campaign to promote 'British values'. Indeed, there is a legal obligation on schools and colleges to promote this particular myth! The Counter-Terrorism and Security Act 2015 lays a duty upon colleges and schools to ensure that children and young people are not drawn into terrorism and an integral part of this strategy is to see that they learn about the values supposedly contained in the Magna Carta, thus guaranteeing that the next generation will also embrace this particular idea in years to come.

The wonderful thing about the peculiarly British mythic archetypes which we have examined in this book is that they provide a ready-made vehicle for the hopes, fears and prejudices of each succeeding generation. They scarcely even need any tweaking from century to century. Take the 'Invaders from the East', surely one of the most popular of these myths.

From the Battle of Hastings to the Spanish Armada, from Waterloo to the Battle of Britain; the essential form of this threat has remained unchanged. It consists of the image of hordes of foreigners heading towards the English

Channel with the intention of coming ashore in Britain and taking over the country. The most recent incarnation of this myth may be seen in the columns of refugees trekking through the Balkans from Greece, having made their way from Syria, Afghanistan and Africa with the supposed intention of coming to Britain. The so-called 'Jungle' camp at Calais struck such a powerful chord among British people for the same reason – that it resonated with this ancient part of the British mythos. Here were the swarthy invaders, camped on our very doorstep, just waiting to cross the Channel to Britain!

What of the other mythic themes at which we have been looking? In 2016, a referendum was held in the United Kingdom on the future of the nation's relationship with Europe. For a little over forty years, the country had flirted with the idea of being part of the Continent, as had been the case for many centuries, from the Iron Age Celts to the Plantagenet monarchy. This has now come to an end and Britain seems set once again to be an island nation. It is intriguing to see how immigration played a leading role in this decision, the 'Invaders from the East' supposedly marching towards the channel prompting over seventeen million people to vote to sever links with the rest of Europe.

Of one thing we may be very sure and that is that the uniquely British mythos we have examined in this book will still be influencing those living in the country for the foreseeable future. The templates for analysing and interpreting Britain's situation and future have proved exceedingly durable and are unlikely to fade away any time soon.

Bibliography

Alexander, Caroline, *The Bounty: The True Story of the Mutiny on the Bounty*, London, HarperCollins, 2003.

Barraclough, Geoffrey, *The Times Concise Atlas of World History*, London, Times Books, 1982.

Brewer, Paul, *The Chronicles of War*, London, Carlton Books, 2007.

Briggs, Asa, *A Social History of England*, New York, The Viking Press, 1983.

Canning, John, *100 Great Lives*, London, Souvenir Press, 1975.

Cawthorne, Nigel, *Kings and Queens of England*, London, Arcturus Publishing, 2010.

Clark, Alan, *The Donkeys*, London, Hutchinson, 1961.

Cook, Chris, and Stevenson, John, *The Longman Handbook of Modern British History 1714-1980*, Harlow, Longman Group, 1983.

Cornwell, Bernard, *Waterloo: The True Story of Four Days, Three Armies and Three Battles*, London, William Collins, 2014.

Cotterell, Arthur, and Storm, Rachel, *The Encyclopaedia of World Mythology*, London, Anness Publishing, 1999.

Cowley, Robert (ed.), *What If? Military Historians Imagine What Might Have Been*, New York, Penguin Putnam, 1999.

Cronin, Vincent, *Napoleon*, Glasgow, Fontana, 1971.

Crystal, David (ed.), *The Cambridge Biographical Encyclopaedia*, Cambridge, Cambridge University Press, 1994.

Dakers, Caroline, *The Blue Plaque Guide to London*, London, The Macmillan Press, 1981.

Fountain, Nigel (ed.), *The Battle of Britain and the Blitz*, London, Michael O'Mara Books, 2002.

Fremont-Barnes, Geoffrey, *Waterloo 1815*, Stroud, The History Press, 2012.

Frey, Hugo, *101 Key Ideas in History*, London, Hodder Headline, 2002.

Garnett, Mark, and Weight, Richard, *Modern British History*, London, Pimlico, 2004.

Glover, Michael, *Battlefields of Northern France and the Low Countries*, London, Michael Joseph, 1987.

Gogerly, Liz, *Who Was Florence Nightingale?*, London, Wayland, 2007.

Halle, Kay, *The Irrepressible Churchill*, London, Conway, 1985.

Harris, Melvin, *Book of Firsts*, London, Michael O'Mara Books, 1994.

Hasek, Jaroslav, translated by Cecil Parrot, *The Good Soldier Svejk*, London, Penguin Books, 1973.

Howse, Christopher, *How We Saw It: 1855-2005*, London, Ebury Press, 2004.

Jerome, Jerome K., *Three Men in a Boat*, London, J. W. Arrowsmith, 1889.

Marriot, Emma, *Bad History; How We Got the Past Wrong*, London, Michael O'Mara Books, 2011.

Morgan, Kenneth (ed.), *The Young Oxford History of Britain and Ireland*, Oxford, Oxford University Press, 1996.

Neville, Peter, *Russia: A Complete History*, London, Windrush Press, 2002.

Palmer, Alan, *The Penguin Dictionary of Modern History*, London, Cresset Press, 1962.

Perkin, Joan, *Victorian Women*, London, John Murray, 1993.

Priestly, J.B., *The Edwardians*, London, William Heinemann, 1970.

Regan, Geoffrey, *The Guinness Book of Military Blunders*, London, Guinness Publishing, 1991.

Regan, Geoffrey, *Naval Blunders*, London, Guinness Publishing, 1993.

Regan, Geoffrey, *Air Force Blunders*, London, Carlton Books, 2002.

Segal, Robert A., *Myth; A Very Short Introduction*, Oxford, Oxford University Press, 2004.

Sellar, W.C., and Yeatman, R.J., *1066 and All That*, London, Methuen, 1930.

Simons, Paul, *Since Records Began*, London, HarperCollins, 2008.

Small, Hugh, *Florence Nightingale: Avenging Angel*, London, Palgrave MacMillan, 1999.

Standage, Tom, *The Victorian Internet: The Remarkable Story of the Telegraph and the Nineteenth Century's Online Pioneers*, London, Weidenfeld & Nicolson, 1998.

Taylor, A.J.P., *The First World War; An Illustrated History*, London, Hamish Hamilton, 1963.

Tombs, Robert, *The English and Their History*, London, Penguin Books, 2014.

Toye, Richard, *Lloyd George and Churchill*, London, Macmillan, 2007.

Tressell, Robert, *The Ragged Trousered Philanthropists*, London, Grant Richards, 2014.

Vallence, Edward, *A Radical History of Britain*, London, Little Brown, 2009.

Webb, Simon, *Dynamite, Treason and Plot: Terrorism in Victorian and Edwardian London*, Stroud, The History Press, 2012.

Webb, Simon, *The Suffragette Bombers; Britain's Unknown Terrorists*, Barnsley, Pen & Sword Books, 2014.

Index